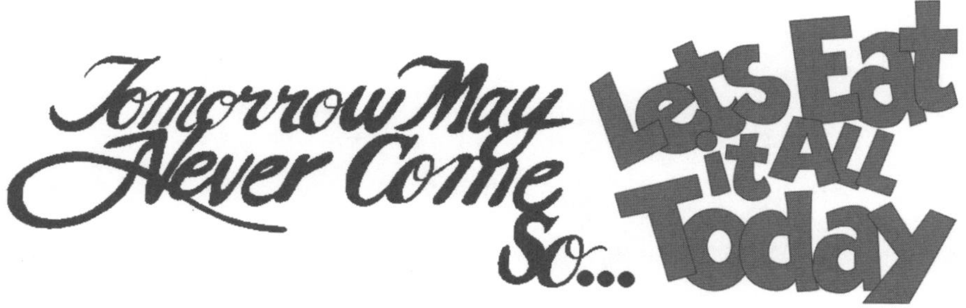

Published By Sharon Strickland and Rosemary Newman
Authors of Southern Ladies Know How to Cook It!
Tea Time Southern Style: Did Someone Say Tea?

Library of Congress #2002092324

Printed By Square One Graphics, Inc.
Second Printing
Cover Illustration By: The Saratoga Group
Cover Design By: Randy Pitt
Contents Designed By: Avonne Beaver
Illustrations By: Cheryl Pierce and Avonne Beaver

Going through life, one of God's greatest blessings is sending us special friends. Throughout this book, you'll see how blessed we've been by how many friends shared their most precious recipes with us. We wish to thank them all.

We offer special thanks to one of our most dearest, dearest friends, Lynette Wright, who recently lost her beloved mother and honored some of her mother's favorite recipes. Lynette's mother, Helen, was an excellent cook, a wonderful, loving wife and mother. She was a member of the Eastern Star and along with her husband, Sam, helped burned and crippled children for many years. Her name will appear at the bottom of her recipes.

We also extend much appreciation to:

The Red Lion - Stockbridge, Massachusetts
Lovanna and George Harvey - Fort Worth, Texas
Donna Durgin - Woodstock, Vermont
Barbara Forrister - Darien, Georgia
Jane Doogin - Birmingham, Alabama
Vagnita Morris - New Port News, Virginia
Barbara Farris and Joan C. Neuger - Wadsworth, Ohio
and to all others that contributed their time and effort.

May God Bless,
Sharon and Rose

My mother-in-law, Nova was a good country cook and could prepare a meal fit for a king. She had a wonderful sense of humor and could tell a joke like no one else. The thing I remember most of all about Nova was the big music box with the large tin records. She would put the records on and dance around the room. We never realize how much someone could be missed until they're gone. Nova, I miss you. This book would be right up your alley.

Nova Newman

Love,
Rose

In Loving Memory

Esther Strickland, "Granny", as I called her wasn't the typical mother-in-law. She was a genuine friend as well as my second mom. She was wise, soft-spoken and just plain enjoyable to be around. She helped me make it through my mom's death. She and I would cook together when we'd visit. She always liked for me to make the chicken and pastry (dumplins to me). We shared so many conversations in both of our kitchens, as well as laughter. She made my life a happier place, and I'm thankful to God, He allowed me to share part of her life.

Esther Strickland

With love,
Sharon

Do You Know How Good It Feels?

Do you know how good it feels to wake up in the morning?
To have spring pounce upon you without any warning
To see bees as they go about their duty
To see Easter lilies in all of their beauty
To watch as the trees bring forth new life
To watch roses bloom, oh what a sight
All of these things we may take for granted
Our Father alone, he sowed and he planted
To make us feel good when we wake in the morning
To let spring come upon us without any warning
He let us see bees as they go about their duty
We saw Easter lilies in all of their beauty
We watched as the trees brought about new life
We watched roses bloom, oh what a sight
We thank you Father for all you have done
For all your hard work and your beautiful son.

Rose

CEP

Appetizers, Soups & Salads

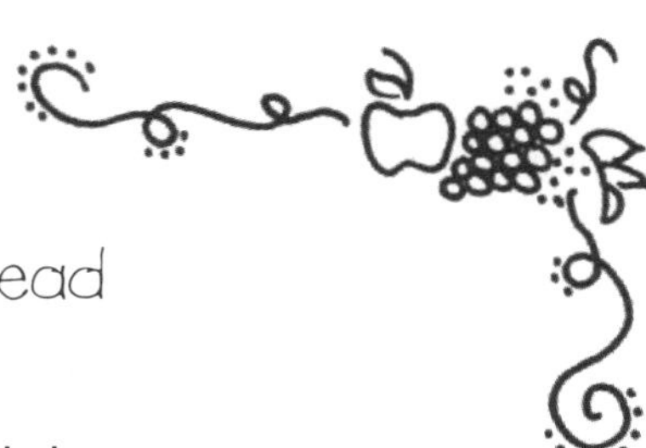

Salmon Spread

1 can salmon, deboned
2-8 ounce packages cream cheese
3/4 cup chopped green onions with blades
2 tablespoons lemon juice
hot pepper sauce to taste

Combine all ingredients in a food processor and puree. Pour into a decorative small bowl (2 cups). Cover and refrigerate overnight.

Cheese Ball

2-8 ounce packages cream cheese
1 small can crushed pineapple, drained
1 teaspoon seasoned salt
2 teaspoons green pepper, finely chopped
1 teaspoon onion, grated
1 1/2 cups chopped nuts

Mix cheese and pineapple. Add salt, pepper, onions and 1/2 cup nuts for inside of ball. Roll ball in remaining nuts. Yields: 1 large ball or 2 small ones.

Ham Cheese Ball

1-8 ounce cream cheese, softened
1/4 cup mayonnaise
2 cups ham, chopped
1/2 cup parsley, chopped
chopped pecans to garnish
1/2 cup green onions
1/4 teaspoon Tabasco
1/4 teaspoon dry mustard

Form ingredients into a ball. Chill. Roll in chopped pecans.

Cheese Krispies

1 stick margarine
1 cup cheddar cheese
1 cup self-rising flour
1 cup Rice Krispies
dash of red pepper

Cream margarine and cheese. Add other ingredients. Bake at 400 degrees for 12 minutes.

Smoked Cheese Ball

1-8 ounce package cheddar cheese
1-8 ounce package cream cheese
1 package smoked cheese spread
1 teaspoon dry mustard
2 teaspoons Worcestershire sauce
1 can black olives, drained and chopped

Grate cheddar cheese. Soften cream cheese and smoked cheese spread. Mix cheeses together. Add dry mustard and chopped olives. Mix well and shape into balls. Sprinkle with parsley.

Hot Sausage and Cheese Puffs

I pound hot Italian or sweet sausage
3 cups Bisquick baking mix
I pound sharp cheddar cheese, shredded
3/4 cup water

Cook meat in a skillet, breaking with a fork, 8-10 minutes. Drain off fat. Spoon sausage into a large bowl. Cool completely. Add the cheese, Bisquick mix and water. Mix with fork until blended. Roll into 1" balls; place on large cookie sheet. Bake at 400 degrees for 15 minutes or until puffed and brown. May be reheated in foil. These are very tasty - even the next day. Yields 50 servings.

Potato Cheese Balls

2 cups mashed potatoes
3 tablespoons cream
Cubed cheese (your choice)
I tablespoon margarine
I egg
salt to taste

Melt butter. To potatoes, add margarine, cream, salt and egg. Beat well. Form into small balls and dent a hollow in each ball and insert a cheese cube. Roll in melted butter and bake in preheated 450 degree oven until brown.

Barbecued Pecans

2 teaspoons garlic salt
1/4 pound butter
2 teaspoons Tabasco sauce
2 tablespoons Worcestershire sauce
1 1/2 pounds pecan halves

Put garlic salt, Worcestershire sauce, butter and Tabasco in a skillet. Warm and mix well. Stir in pecans. Then pour onto cookie sheet or into a shallow baking pan. Bake for 30 minutes at 250 degrees. Remove from oven and stir. Bake again for 30 minutes. Then turn out on wax paper to cool. Can be stored for weeks in jars, tins, etc.

Cheese Spread

2 pounds New York cream cheese or aged cheddar
1 teaspoon salt
1/2 cup catsup
1/2 cup A-1 or Lea & Perrin sauce
1 teaspoon mustard
1/2 teaspoon red pepper
2 tablespoons Worcestershire sauce
5 shakes Tabasco sauce
1 cup beer
1/2 cup parsley, chopped fine

Grind cheese and add ingredients in order given. Beat very thoroughly until mixture is smooth. Store in refrigerator in sealed container. Can be kept a long time (if you can hide it). Makes an excellent stuffing for celery, or cheese spread for Melba toast, potato chips or crackers.

Barnard Inn Cheese Dip

2 1/2 pounds medium cheddar, finely chopped
2 stalks celery, finely chopped
1/2 cup onion
5 medium cloves garlic, crushed
3 tablespoons Worcestershire sauce
1 1/2 cup sour cream
2/3 teaspoons black ground pepper
1 teaspoon paprika
sherry

Grate cheese, put in mixing bowl and add all the ingredients except for sherry. Mix with dough hook. Mix well, then add sherry until dip has right (spreadable) consistency. Better if refrigerated overnight.

from the kitchen of Sepp Schenkar

Garlic Butter

1 pound unsalted butter (room temperature)
4 cloves garlic, crushed
juice of one lemon
1 tablespoon mustard
1 tablespoon Worcestershire sauce
1/2 teaspoon black ground pepper
1 heaping tablespoon fresh parsley, finely chopped

Put all ingredients in mixing bowl and mix-whip to slightly fluffy. Keeps for two weeks in refrigerator or freeze in small portions. Has many uses such as sauteeing shrimp, veal or chicken, or on top of steak or fish.

from the kitchen of Donna Durgin

Cream of Onion

Chop onions; saute in butter, deglaze with dry wine. Top off with good chicken or duck stock (enough liquid to cover the onions) and add some grated nutmeg. Simmer for approximately one hour. Thicken lightly with a mix of 1/3 cornstarch, 2/3 flour. Then add half and half and whisk well, so no lumps remain. Add to soup carefully. Add a little heavy cream 5 minutes before serving.

from the kitchen of Donna Durgin

Bacon Cheese Dip

2 cups cheddar cheese, shredded
3 green onions (use stems), chopped
8 slices bacon, fried crisp and crumbled
1/4 cup slivered almonds
mayonnaise (enough to mix)

Mix all ingredients. Refrigerate 24 hours. Add more mayonnaise, if necessary, when ready to serve. Use as a dip for crackers or large Fritos.

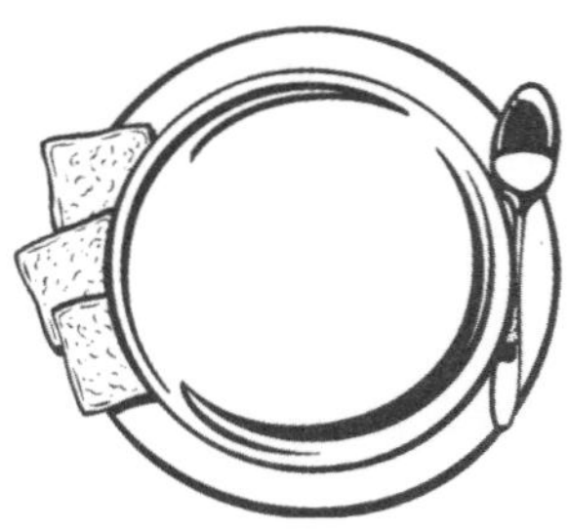

Ham and Vegetable Chowder

2 tablespoons unsalted butter
1 cup fresh, dry yellow onion, diced
2 chicken bouillon cubes
1 cup water
2 cups small diced fresh red potatoes
1-10 ounce package frozen mixed vegetables
1-10 ounce package frozen corn
1 ounce all-purpose flour
4 cups half and half
2 1/2 cups small cured ham, diced
(suggested: Honey Baked Ham brand)
salt and pepper to taste
(suggested: cayenne)

In a large casserole or saucepan (preferably stainless steel), melt butter. Add the onion and cook, stirring over moderate heat until softened but not browned - about three minutes.

Crumble the bouillon cubes over the onion and add the water to the mixture. Stir in the potatoes, mixed vegetables and corn. Cover and cook, stirring occasionally, until the vegetables are tender - about 20 minutes.

In a medium bowl, whisk the flour with 1/4 cup of the half and half until smooth and creamy. Blend in the remaining half and half gradually, to avoid forming lumps, then pour the half and half mixture into a large saucepan and cook until thickened slightly, about 5 minutes. Stir the milk mixture and ham into the vegetables. Simmer, uncovered, stirring frequently, for about fifteen minutes. Add salt and pepper to taste.

from the kitchen of Lovanna and George Harvey

Steak Soup

1 1/2 pound steak, cubed
4 tablespoons butter
1-16 ounce can tomatoes, diced
3 tablespoons beef base (Schilling's)
1 teaspoon salt
1 teaspoon pepper
1 cup celery, chopped
1-10 ounce package frozen mixed vegetables
1 cup onion, chopped
1 cup carrots, chopped
1/2 cup soft oleo
1 1/2 cup flour
2 cups water

Brown steak in 4 tablespoons butter. Add 6 cups water, tomatoes, beef base, salt and pepper. Bring to a boil; cover and reduce heat. Simmer for 30 minutes. Add mixed vegetables, celery, onions and carrots. Continue to simmer, covered, for another 30 minutes. Combine 1/2 cup oleo and flour. Gradually blend in 2 cups water. Add to meat; mix, cook and stir until mixture is thick and bubbly.

Potato Soup

6 medium potatoes, diced
2 tablespoons butter
2 carrots, diced
1/4 cup onion, finely chopped
2 tablespoons flour
1 quart milk
1 tablespoon salt
1/4 teaspoon tarragon
1/4 teaspoon basil
1/4 teaspoon Accent
1 chicken bouillon cube

Cook potatoes in boiling, salted water until tender. Melt butter in large kettle; add carrots and onion. Cover and cook until tender. Remove from heat; add flour. Stir in milk. Add 1/2 of the potatoes. Mash the rest of the potatoes and add with rest of ingredients. Heat until steaming, but not boiling.

French Onion Soup

3 medium sweet onions
2 tablespoons olive oil plus extra for brushing
1 teaspoon mustard seed
1 teaspoon celery seed
1 teaspoon cracked black pepper
4 cups beef stock
1/4 cup red wine
1 teaspoon Worcestershire sauce
1 large Portobella mushroom
3 slices gruyere or provolone cheese
salt and pepper to taste

Slice onions very thin. Place a 5 quart stockpot over medium-high heat. Add olive oil and onions. After about 10 minutes, lower heart to medium-low. Add salt and pepper to taste, mustard seed, celery seed and cracked pepper. Continue to saute another 20-25 minutes or until the onions are carmelized to deep golden brown. When onions are rich brown, add beefstock, wine and Worcestershire sauce. Turn heat up to medium and cook 15 minutes. Preheat broiler.

In meantime, cut stem off mushroom. Place mushroom on side and slice into 4 thin pieces. Heat a large skillet over medium-high heat. Brush mushroom slices with olive oil and place in skillet, cooking for a couple of minutes on each side, till lightly browned.

Ladel soup into 4 (oven safe) bowls. Place mushroom slice on top; add a slice of cheese on top of mushroom. Place bowls on cookie sheet and place under broiler until cheese gets bubbly and brown. Best to use stoneware or other oven safe bowls for cheese to brown properly.

Yields: 4 servings.

from the kitchen of Lynette Wright

Rose's Vegetable Soup In A Hurry

I pound ground beef
2 cans tomato soup
2 medium potatoes
I large onion
I can whole kernel corn
I/2 package frozen peas
I/4 package frozen carrots
I hot peppper
2 tablespoons sugar
salt and pepper to taste

Brown ground beef in skillet. Drain and set aside. In large saucepan combine potatoes and onion. Add enough water to cover; boil for 3 minutes. Empty 2 cans of tomato soup, whole kernel corn, frozen peas, carrots, hot pepper, sugar, salt and pepper into potatoes and onion. Add ground beef. Cover with lid. Cook on medium heat, stirring about every 5 minutes for 30 minutes. Very Good.

Three-Day Cole Slaw

1 cabbage head
1 or 2 onions, if small
2/3 cup vinegar
1 cup sugar
1/2 cup oil
1 tablespoon mustard
  (prepared is OK)
1 tablespoon celery seed
1 tablespoon salt

Combine sugar, vinegar, mustard, oil and celery seed. Bring to a boil. Cool. Alternate cabbage and onions and pack in wide mouth jar. Then pour oil dressing over cabbage (run a knife blade around sides to let oil get to bottom). Set in refrigerator overnight at least. Yields: 1 quart of cole slaw.

Salad Nicoise

crisp salad greens
hard cooked eggs, sliced
anchovy fillets
sliced, cold potatoes,
  marinated in oil and vinegar
sliced, peeled tomatoes or
  tiny cherry tomatoes
thin green pepper rings
tuna
tiny ripe olives
cold cooked green beans
capers
onion rings
Cressioniere Sauce
2 teaspoons fresh basil

Arrange greens on large platter. Arrange slices of egg on top of greens and top each slice with a curled anchovy. Add marinated potatoes and remaining ingredients except Cressioniere Sauce and basil. Serve with Cressioniere Sauce (see recipe below) flavored with basil.

Cressoniere Sauce:

Combine 1/2 cup olive oil and 3 tablespoons vinegar; beat until well blended. Season with salt and pepper; add 1 hard cooked egg and 2 chopped tablespoons of watercress. This salad may be used as a meal for lunch or the salad course for dinner. Ingredients may vary accordingly.

Sauerkraut Salad

1-11 pound 11 ounce can sauerkraut
3/4 cup sugar
1 cup celery, diced
1 cup green pepper, diced
1/4 cup onion, diced
3 tablespoons vinegar
1/2 teaspoon salt
1/8 teaspoon pepper
1 teaspoon celery seeds
3 tablespoons diced pimiento

Drain sauerkraut in colander for 15 minutes. Cut into 1" pieces and place in large mixing bowl. Add remaining ingredients and mix well. Store, covered, in refrigerator at least 24 hours. Makes10 servings.

Cauliflower Salad

4 cups cauliflower, thinly sliced
2/3 cup green pepper, chopped
1/2 cup onion, chopped
1 cup ripe olives, chopped
1/2 cup pimiento, chopped

Mix the above ingredients into a bowl.

Dressing:

1/2 cup salad oil
3 tablespoons wine vinegar
1 tablespoon sugar
3 tablespoons lemon juice
2 teaspoons salt
1/4 teaspoon pepper

Mix in a blender, pour over salad and let stand 24 hours or longer. The taste improves with age. Serves 10 to 12.

Crunchy Cauliflower Salad

1 medium head cauliflower
1 cup radishes, sliced (optional)
1/2 cup green onions, sliced
1-8 ounce can water chestnuts, sliced and drained
3/4 cup sour cream
3/4 cup mayonnaise
2 tablespoons caraway seeds
1 0.37 ounce package buttermilk salad dressing mix
salt and pepper to taste

Wash the cauliflower and break into flowerets. Combine cauliflower and next three ingredients in a medium mixing bowl; toss gently. Stir together remaining ingredients; pour over vegetables and stir well. Spoon into serving bowl; cover and chill before serving.

from the kitchen of Lovanna and George Harvey

Macaroni Cheese Salad

1-8 ounce box elbow macaroni
2 green peppers, seeded and diced
1 cup cheddar cheese, diced
1/3 cup green onions, sliced
2/3 cup mayonnaise
1/3 cup sour cream
1 teaspoon salt
1/4 teaspoon pepper
1 tablespoon lemon juice
olives (optional)

Cook macaroni according to directions. Drain and rinse with cold water to stop the cooking action. Put macaroni in large bowl; add diced green peppers, cheese, onions, olives, mayonnaise, sour cream, salt, pepper and lemon juice. Mix thoroughly and chill for several hours to blend flavors. Serves 6 to 8.

from the kitchen of JD

Frozen Cole Slaw

2 heads cabbage
4 carrots
2 sweet peppers (red or green)
2 tablespoons salt
4 cups white sugar
1 1/2 cup water
1 1/2 cup vinegar
2 teaspoons mustard seed
1 teaspoon celery seed (optional)

Shred cabbage and carrots. Dice sweet peppers. Mix together with salt and let stand for one hour in refrigerator.

Combine sugar, water, vinegar, mustard and celery seed in a pan. Boil quickly, just until sugar dissolves. Let cool. Pour syrup over the vegetables and mix well. Pack in freezer containers. Seal and freeze. Store at 0 degrees to 18 degrees c.

Spinach Salad

1 package fresh spinach, diced
5 or 6 hard cooked eggs, diced
1 pound bacon, crumbled
1 can bean sprouts, drained
1 cup fresh sliced mushrooms (optional)

Mix well and serve chilled.

Cherry Salad

16 ounce dark sweet pitted cherries
8 ounce cream cheese
8 ounce pineapple
2 cups minature marshmallows
1/2 cup walnuts
1 package Dream Whip, prepared as directed

Cream the cream cheese with 1/4 cup cherry juice from can of cherries. Mix in drained fruit and nuts. Fold Dream Whip into mixture. Pour into serving bowl and chill for 8 hours.

Lime Salad

1 package lime jello
1 dozen marshmallows
1 1/2 cups boiling water
1 small can crushed pineapple
1 small package cream cheese
1 cup nuts
3 rounded tablespoons mayonnaise
1 cup thickly whipped cream

Dissolve jello and marshmallows in boiling water. Let cool slightly and add cream cheese. Beat with egg beater to get cheese dissolved. Add crushed pineapple, nuts and mayonnaise. Chill until slightly thick, then fold in whipped cream. Chill.

Cole Slaw

Shred one large head of cabbage and soak in ice water until crisp (overnight if possible). Drain well and add 2 large onions cut in thin rings; over this pour the following Cole Slaw Dressing:

Cole Slaw Dressing

2 teaspoons salt
4 small garlic buds, crushed
1/4 cup vinegar
1/8 cup water
5/8 cup salad oil

Blend salt with crushed garlic. Add liquid and shake vigorously to blend thoroughly. Pour over prepared cabbage and toss lightly.

Frozen Strawberry Salad

8 ounce package cream cheese
3/4 cup sugar
1 large can pineapple tidbits, drained
1-10 ounce package frozen strawberries
2 bananas, sliced
1/2 cup chopped nuts
1 large container of Cool Whip

Beat cream cheese with sugar, creaming well. In another bowl, mix pineapple tidbits, strawberries, bananas, nuts and Cool Whip. Mix thoroughly but gently. Combine this with cream cheese mixture. Spoon into loaf pan and freeze overnight. Makes 12 to 14 servings.

Note: This keeps from 4 to 6 weeks in the freezer. Lining the pan with waxed paper makes it easier to lift out.

Sauces & Dressings

In August of 2001, while visiting Key West, Florida, my husband, Paul, our dear friends, Lester and Glenda Claxton and myself, decided to go to Margaritaville. Much to our surprise and enjoyment, they had a special guest named the "Sauce Boss". He was one of the most delightful and refreshing people we had ever met, and to top it off he was a magnificent cook as well.

Bill, "The Sauce Boss" Wharton's Gumbo was the best we'd ever eaten. He also played the meanest guitar in the land. We returned everynight for the next three nights staying until 2:00 am. We couldn't resist the opportunity to stir the gumbo. Now, this wasn't good for our diets, but it sure was good for our appetites.

"The Sauce Boss" is well known for his hot sauces that he puts in his gumbo. Following this story you will find his famous recipe that you too can enjoy. To get your hot sauce to go in the recipe, you can find it online at sauceboss.com or come on by "Southern Ladies Hidden Treasures" in Savannah, Georgia, and we'll be glad to sell you some. It's the meanest hot sauce in the world. Who knows, we might even let you stir the gumbo?

Happy Cookin'
Rose Newman

Sauce Boss Gumbo

Make A Roux:

Mix:

2 cups of flour into 1 1/2 cups hot oil.

Cook on high, stirring constantly until brown.

Add:

1 chicken, cooked and de-boned
1 gallon of chicken stock
2 large onions
2 large green peppers.

Bring to a boil, then simmer down.

Add:

salt to taste
1/2 cup of...(drum roll) Bill Wharton's Liquid Summer Hot Sauce

Slice & Add:

1 pound of smoked sausage
2 medium zucchini
1 pound of okra

When the okra is done, bring the gumbo to a rolling boil.

Add:

1 pound shrimp
1 pint of oysters
1 pound of crawdads.

Cook for 3 minutes

Serve over rice and splash with Liquid Summer Hot Sauce.

As time
goes on...
& on...
& on...

Sausage Saw Mill Gravy

In Loving Memory of Aunt Kansas Shular

1 pound sausage
flour (self-rising or plain)
salt
pepper
milk

Crumble sausage in heavy frying pan and cook until well browned. Remove sausage and set aside. Add small amounts of flour, stirring constantly, to hot grease until it becomes thick and brown (about 4 tablespoons). Add salt and pepper to taste (about 1 tablespoon each). Add milk slowly until desired thickness (about 4 cups average).

Aunt Kansas was a great country cook. She raised four children and cooked for at least a half dozen more every Saturday morning. That was "Saw Mill Gravy Time."

Aunt Kansas and Uncle Carl had milk cows so the milk was always fresh and the eggs came straight out of the yard. She made big cathead biscuits to go with the gravy. We hope you enjoy her recipe and make wonderful memories like the ones that we have.

We miss you Aunt Kansas.

If someone
picked
your
daisies.
Go
bake a
pie.
Rose

Cucumber and Yogurt Sauce

1 large cucumber
1 cup plain yogurt
1 teaspoon vegetable oil
1/2 teaspoon garlic, chopped
salt to taste

Cut the cucumber in half. Remove seeds and chop. Add remaining ingredients. Mix well. Excellent with hot spicy buffalo wings.

Unusual Dressing

(most unusual taste, but delicious)

1/2 cup salad oil
1/3 cup catsup
1/3 cup sugar
1/4 cup vinegar
1 teaspoon each salt and pepper
1/2 teaspoon dry mustard
2 teaspoons onion, grated
1 1/2 teaspoons bottled steak sauce
1 clove garlic, minced

Combine and blend thoroughly with electric or rotary beater. Makes 1 1/3 cups.

from the kitchen of Lynette Wright

Marinara Sauce

2 pints canned diced tomatoes
2 tablespoons olive oil
1 teaspoon fresh chopped garlic
1 3/4 teaspoons oregano (dried)
3 tablespoons fresh chopped parsley
salt and pepper to taste

In a saucepan, cook until liquid has evaporated to half, stirring so as not to scorch. In frying pan, heat the oil and add garlic. Don't overcook; will burn. Pour into tomatoes along with remaining ingredients. Stir. Cook on low heat for 5 minutes.

Red Tomato Catsup

1 1/2 gallon strained tomato juice
4 cups vinegar
3 cups sugar
1/2 cup salt
1/2 cup grated horse radish
1/2 cup ground mustard
1 teaspoon red pepper
1 teaspoon whole cloves
1 teaspoon cinnamon

Put all spices in a bag and boil in the tomato juice until juice is thick. Remove bag and continue cooking until desired thickness. Seal in air tight jars.

Potato and Garlic Mayonnaise

2 large potatoes, peeled and cubed
1 teaspoon garlic powder
2 teaspoons paprika
2 egg yolks
2 teaspoons water
salt and pepper to taste
1 cup olive oil

In saucepan, cook potato until done. Drain, then whip with electric mixer. Add next 5 ingredients and whip. Gradually add oil; makes about 1 1/2 cups.

Thousand Island Dressing

1 cup mayonnaise
3 tablespoons vinegar
2 teaspoons sugar
1/4 cup catsup
2 tablespoons pickle, chopped
1 egg, chopped

Mix all ingredients together and chill.

Swiss Cheese Sauce

3 tablespoons butter
3 tablespoons flour
2 cups milk
salt and pepper to taste
1 cup swiss cheese, grated

Melt the butter over low heat. Add the flour, stirring with fork. Do not brown. Add the milk, stirring quickly and constantly. Stir and cook 4-5 minutes until smooth. When cooked remove from heat; stir in cheese until smooth.

Vinaigrette Dressing

2 tablespoons red wine or cider vinegar
6 tablespoons olive or peanut oil
salt and pepper to taste
parsley
basil
thyme

Mix well. Refrigerate short time. Pour over green salad or California Salad.

Helen's Spaghetti Sauce

1 large onion, chopped
1 cup celery, chopped
1/4 teaspoon bell pepper, chopped
1/2 teaspoon sugar
1/2 teaspoon chili powder
1/2 teaspoon paprika powder
1/8 teaspoon garlic powder (or 3 good shakes)
1 tablespoon Worcestershire sauce
1/2 bay leaf
1/2 teaspoon parsley flakes
1 #303 can tomatoes
1-15 ounce can tomato sauce
1-3 ounce can tomato paste
1-4 ounce can chopped mushrooms
1 package spaghetti sauce mix
1 cup american cheese, cubed
1 pork chop for each person to be served
salt and pepper pork chops
Water, if needed, during cooking

Brown chops in small amount of oil and set aside. Wilt onions, celery, and bell peppers. Add all except cheese and chops. Cook at least 30 minutes stirring often to prevent sticking. Add chops and cook until tender. Add cheese about 15 minutes before turning off. Sauce is even better the next day, if there is any left.

from the kitchen of Helen

Cream Sauce with Ham

1/2 pound cooked ham (sliced ham can be used), cubed
2 tablespoons plus 1 teaspoon butter
2 tablespoons flour
1 cup milk
1/2 teaspoon grated nutmeg
salt and pepper
1 tablespoon shallots, chopped
3 tablespoons sherry wine
2-4 slices buttered toast

Set aside ham cubes. Heat 2 tablespoons of butter in sauce pan and add flour. Stir with wire whisk. When blended, add milk, stirring rapidly with whisk. Add nutmeg; salt and pepper to taste. Bring to boil; let cook for 5 minutes.

In skillet heat butter and add ham. Cook briefly, stirring constantly. Stir in sherry. Heat throughly. Add cream sauce to skillet and turn off heat. Stir well to blend. Spoon over toast.

Serves 2-4.

Lemon Butter Sauce

1 cup butter
1 lemon (juiced)
2 cloves of garlic crushed left in peeling
2 teaspoons Worcestershire sauce
salt to taste

Melt butter, getting hot but not bubbling. Add remaining ingredients and stir. Heat until very hot. Discard the garlic.

Cooked Salad Dressing

1 tablespoon flour
1/2 cup sugar
1 teaspoon salt
1 teaspoon dry mustard
1/4 teaspoon paprika
dash of pepper
2 eggs, well beaten
1/2 cup vinegar
3/4 cup water
1 tablespoon butter

Combine dry ingredients; add water, vinegar and eggs. Blend well; place over low heat and stir constantly until thick. Remove from heat and stir in butter.

Mushroom Sauce

3 tablespoons butter
1 1/2 tablespoons green onions, finely chopped
2 cups sliced mushrooms
salt and pepper to taste
1 cup canned diced tomatoes
1/2 cup dry white wine
1/2 cup whipping cream
2 tablespoons fresh parsley, chopped

Melt butter and saute onions until almost transparent. Add the mushrooms, salt and pepper and cook until all liquid evaporates. Add the tomatoes and cook until hot. Stir in the wine and cook about 5 minutes more. Add the cream. Allow to boil for 60 seconds more. Stir in parsley.

Chocolate Fudge Sauce

1 cup semisweet chocolate chips
1 stick butter or margarine
1 can evaporated milk
1-16 ounce package powdered sugar

Melt butter and chocolate chips. Add milk and sugar. Stir vigorously. Bring to full boil. Simmer for about 5 minutes. Let cool. Serve over ice cream, pancakes or your choice of foods.

Bearnaise Sauce

Glaze:

1 1/2 tablespoons green shallot (scallion) tops, finely chopped
1/4 teaspoon minced garlic
2 teaspoon lemon juice
1/4 cup dry white wine
1/2 tablespoon dried tarragon
1/2 tablespoon dried chervil
1/8 teaspoon salt
1/4 teaspoon white pepper

1/2 cup salt butter
3 large egg yolks
1/8 teaspoon (scant) cayenne

In a small heavy saucepan, combine the ingredients for the glaze and cook over medium heat until the mixture is reduced to about 2 tablespoons; it will have almost no liquid.

In a separate saucepan, melt the butter over medium heat, then remove from the heat. Put the egg yolks and cayenne in the blender. Cover and blend on high for a few seconds. Add the glaze, cover and blend on high for a few seconds longer. Remove the cover, turn on high speed and gradually pour in the hot melted butter in a steady stream.

Cover the blender and switch on for 60 seconds and then off for 30 seconds. Repeat this procedure until the sauce is quite thick. Makes 1 cup of sauce.

Honey Glaze for Ham

1/4 cup honey
1/4 cup soy sauce
1 teaspoon mustard

Mix together. Pour over ham during last 45 minutes of baking.

What Really Makes It Grow

We work so hard to plow the ground
For vegetables to stand
Where mounds of dirt and scattered seed
All flow throughout the land
If we get too busy to thank our Lord
It's important that we know
His sunshine and the wind and rain
Is what really makes it grow.

We look upon you, Lord God
In thanks for what you give
Because of your son, Jesus Christ
We're all allowed to live

One tenth of our harvest is not too much
To ask of us this day
Please bless our families and our fields
For this, Lord God, we pray.

Gina Palmer

Vegetables

If the grass is
greener
on the other
other
side, they
planted
turnip
greens.
Rose

My mother was bedridden for 11 1/2 years. This poem was written shortly before she became totally unable to walk. She never lost her sense of humor, or her sharp mind. She continued to write speeches and poems, which were given by representatives all over the United States, until her death.

Lynette Wright

Growing Old

by Helen H. Jessup

I wake up in the morning,
Put my feet upon the floor,
Every bone in my body aches,
Every muscle seems so sore.

Why does it take so much
pushing?
I'm used to being on the go!
I need to be up and doing,
But for some reason I'm so slow!

There's the house to clean
and polish,
And the washing to be put out,
But my high gears don't seem
to work,
Still in low, I'm getting about.

I make it to the kitchen,
Put the coffee on to brew,
One cup used to send me,
But I now begin with two.

Something definitely is the matter,
But of one fact I am sure,
It certainly isn't a dream
That a little more time
wouldn't cure.

Ye gads, it dawns on me all
of a sudden,
The years have really slipped away,
I look into my mirror,
And find someone old and gray.

Yes, my get up and go has left me,
My spring is really sprung.
But I wouldn't swap my life
and experiences
For a new one that's just begun

For I watch the young folks
scurrying,
Running this way and that.
They can't know where they're
going,
'Cause they don't know where
they're at.

For me, no grumbling, and
a growling,
Nor complaining of the
"might have beens",
I'm thankful that the Lord lets
me linger,
Even in the shape I'm in.

So, I'll sit with my aches and pains,
Watch thru bifocals, as the world
rolls along,
Take time to smell the roses,
Keeping in my heart a song.

A big pot
of
turnips
go good
with
potatoes,
fish &
beans.

Baked Eggplant

1 large eggplant
1/2 medium onion
dash of Worcestershire sauce
butter crackers (not saltines)
1 can cream of mushroom soup
2 tablespoons butter
3 tablespoons chopped parsley
salt and pepper to taste

Cut top off eggplant lengthwise. Scrape out the inside, leaving about 1/2 inch around sides and bottom of shell. Boil eggplant meat in salted water until it is tender. Drain completely and chop. Saute chopped onion in butter and add chopped parsley. Mix with enough crumbled crackers to make a good stuffing consistency. Pile filling back into eggplant shell. Sprinkle with cracker crumbs and dot with butter. Bake at 375 degrees for 30 to 35 minutes.

from the kitchen of Helen

Baked Tomatoes

3 medium tomatoes
1/4 cup Mazola margarine, melted
1/3 cup dry bread crumbs
1 tablespoon brown sugar
1 teaspoon onion, finely chopped
dash pepper

Wash tomatoes, remove stem ends and cut tomatoes in half crosswise. Arrange halves, cut side up, in shallow baking dish. Bake in a 375 degree oven about 15 minutes. Meanwhile, combine remaining ingredients. Spoon onto tomatoes. Broil about 4 inches from heat until tops are nicely browned. Serves 6.

from the kitchen of Helen

Quick Orangey Carrots

5 medium carrots,
cut in thin strips
2 tablespoons orange marmalade
2 tablespoons butter
or margarine

Cook carrots in salted water for 15 to 20 minutes until tender; drain well. Add butter; cover and let stand a few minutes until butter melts. Stir in marmalade to glaze carrots. Serve immediately.

Sweet and Sour Carrots

Cut up carrots and par-boil until tender. Place in buttered dish. Sprinkle with chopped onions and bell pepper.

from the kitchen of Helen

Roasted Vegetable Pasta

2 pounds leeks, with
4 inches of green left on,
quartered lengthwise
1/4 cup olive oil
1/4 cup defatted chicken broth
2 tablespoons fresh thyme leaves
1 tablespoon salt
black pepper to taste
6 ripe plum tomatoes, quartered
2 yellow squash, sliced
into 1/4" rounds
1/2 cup pitted black
olives
1/3 cup flat-leaf
parsley, chopped
1 pound fettuccine,
cooked al dent
parsley

Preheat oven to 400 degrees. Place leeks in a shallow roasting pan and drizzle with olive oil and chicken broth. Sprinkle with thyme, salt and pepper. Cover with aluminum foil; bake for 30 minutes. Remove foil; add tomatoes, squash and olives. Bake, uncovered for 45 minutes or until vegetables are tender. Stir vegetables once or twice. Remove vegetables from oven and adjust seasonings. Toss with parsley and cooked pasta in a large bowl. Serve hot or at room temperature. Serves 6.

Baked Beans

I pound white beans
small bottle catsup
1/2 teaspoon mustard
1/8 cup sugar
1/4 teaspoon pepper
3 tablespoons vinegar
salt to taste
small piece salt pork

Boil beans until tender. Add other ingredients. Fry salt pork and place on top. Pour fat over mixture and bake in 325 degree oven for about an hour. The beans should be very moist (completely covered) when put into the oven.

Peas in Sour Cream Sauce

1-10 ounce package frozen green peas
1 large cucumber, peeled and thinly sliced (1 1/2 cups)
2 tablespoons water
1 teaspoon tarragon leaves
1 teaspoon salt
1/2 cup sour cream
1/2 cup salad dressing
1 tablespoon lemon juice

Combine peas, cucumber, water, tarragon leaves and salt in heavy saucepan. Cover tightly; cook over low heat until peas are tender. Drain and combine sour cream, salad dressing and lemon juice. Warm over very low heat, stirring constantly. Stir peas and cucumbers into sauce and serve immediately.

Makes 4-6 servings.

Yam Town

3 cups mashed sweet potatoes
2 eggs, well beaten
1/2 teaspoons salt
1 can coconut
1 cup sugar
1 teaspoon cinnamon
1/2 cup milk
1 teaspoon vanilla

Mix ingredients and place in baking dish sprayed with Pam.

Topping:

1 stick margarine
1 cup brown sugar
1/2 cup flour
1 teaspoon vanilla
1 cup chopped nuts

Mix well and spread over potato mixture. Cook 40 minutes at 350 degrees.

Zucchini with Apples

2 cups water
1 1/2 pound small zucchini, thinly sliced
1 tablespoon butter
1 medium onion, chopped
2 apples, peeled and chopped
2 tomatoes, peeled and chopped
2 tablespoons fresh parsley, chopped
1/2 teaspoons salt
freshly ground pepper, to taste

In a small saucepan, boil 2 cups water. Drop the zucchini slices into the boiling water for 30 seconds. Remove immediatley and drain. Melt the butter in a large pot and saute onion until transparent. Add apples and stir well. Add tomatoes and blanched zucchini. Stir well, then add parsley. Season with salt and pepper and cook, covered over low heat for 5 to 10 minutes, until the zucchini is soft. Serve hot.

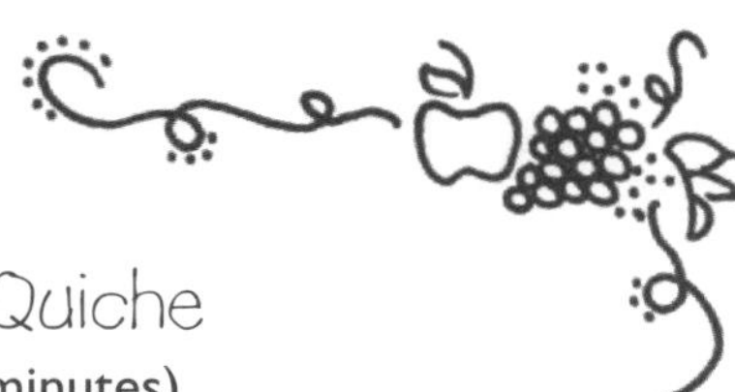

Sweet Onion Quiche

1 (9 inch) pie crust, slightly baked (4 minutes)
1 large Vidalia onion, sliced
1 tablespoon butter or margarine
3 tablespoons flour
1/2 cup sour cream
1/2 cup cottage cheese
1/2 cup milk
2 eggs, slightly beaten
1/2 teaspoon salt

Saute onion slices in butter until soft. Place in pie shell. Mix flour with sour cream. Add other ingredients.

Sweet Onion Pie

1 cup Ritz cracker crumbs
1/4 cup margarine plus 2 tablespoons
2 cups onion, sliced
1/4 cup milk
2 eggs
1/4 teaspoon salt
pepper to taste
grated cheese for top

Melt 1/4 cup margarine and mix with cracker crumbs. Pat into pie shell. Melt 2 tablespoons butter and saute onions until soft. Put in pie shell. Mix eggs, milk and seasonings and pour over onions. Bake 20 minutes at 350 degrees. Add grated cheese and bake 10 minutes more.

Asparagus Casserole

1 can asparagus soup
3 sliced hard-cooked eggs
2 cups cooked rice
grated cheddar cheese

Spread cooked rice in buttered 9 x 13 inch dish. Mix soup and eggs; spread over rice. Sprinkle with cheese. Bake at 375 degrees for 15 minutes.

Cucumber Waltz

1 large or 2 medium cucumbers
1 cup sour cream
1 tablespoon instant minced onion
2 tablespoons vinegar
1 teaspoon salt

Slice unpeeled cucumbers very thin. Combine the other ingredients with the cucumbers. Cover and chill (overnight if possible) before serving.

Corn and Cabbage Casserole

5 slices bacon, diced
1/2 cup liquid from corn
1 can whole kernel corn, drained
2 cups thinly sliced cabbage
1/2 teaspoon salt
1/8 teaspoon pepper
1 teaspoon sugar

Dice bacon and saute until crisp. Remove from pan, reserving 2 or 2 1/2 tablespoons drippings in skillet. Add corn liquid, corn and cabbage to drippings in skillet. Cook covered until cabbage is tender, about 15 to 20 minutes. Add salt, pepper, sugar and bacon. Mix lightly.

Glazed Carrots

1 pound carrots
1 cup water
2-3 tablespoons butter
1 1/2 teaspoon sugar
salt and pepper to taste

Trim and scrape carrots. Cut them 1/8 inch thick. Put carrots in a saucepan and add water. Water should cover carrots. Add butter and sugar; salt and pepper to taste. Cover pan; bring to a boil. Cook 10 minutes. Uncover and cook over high heat until water is gone and carrots are glazed and brown.

Baked Carrots

10 medium-sized carrots
1/2 onion, minced
1/2 cup parsley, minced
1 tablespoon natural sugar
1 teaspoon salt
3 tablespoons oil
1/3 cup boiling water

Wash and scrape carrots lightly; cut in half lengthwise and crosswise. Place in a baking dish. Mix the remaining ingredients, except water. Sprinkle mixture over the carrots, then pour boiling water over all. Cover and bake in 350 degree oven for about an hour and a half.

Green Rice

2 cups hot cooked rice
1/4 cup green onion tops, finely chopped
1/2 cup parsley, finely chopped
4 tablespoons butter

Saute onions in butter for 5 minutes. Add parsley and continue cooking for another 5 minutes. Fold onions, parsley and any remaining butter gently into hot rice and serve.

Corn on the Cob and Peppercorn Butter

8 ears of corn
salt
1/4 cup butter (at room temperature)
1 teaspoon green peppercorn, chopped

Use fresh corn; remove husks and silk from the ears of corn. Use a large kettle of water; bring to boil; add salt. Drop corn into water and cover. Cook about 15 minutes. While corn is cooking, beat butter and green peppercorns together. Chill briefly until firm. This peppercorn butter is also good on other vegetables.

Mac-N-Cheese Southern Style

10 ounces elbow noodles
2 cups sharp cheddar cheese
1 stick butter or margarine
2 tablespoons salt
1 1/2 can evaporated milk

Preheat oven to 350 degrees. Boil noodles until done; drain; add salt. Pour into casserole dish. Slice butter and place all over top of noodles. Slice or grate cheese and spread evenly over top. Add milk. Cook for 30 minutes. Let set 15 minutes.

Cherry Tomatoes with Garlic and Parsley

24 red ripe firm cherry tomatoes
2 tablespoons olive oil
1 teaspoon garlic, finely chopped
2 tablespoons parsley, chopped

Remove stems from tomatoes; rinse and pat dry. Heat oil in 2 quart saucepan. Add tomatoes in one layer about 1-2 minutes, shaking pan to distribute oil around tomatoes. Do not overcook. Sprinkle garlic and parsley over tomatoes. Makes 4 servings.

Asparagus with Parsley and Eggs

21-24 spears of asparagus
salt
one egg
3 tablespoons butter
2-2 1/2 tablespoons parsley, chopped

Put eggs in saucepan and boil 9-10 minutes. Drain and cover with cold water. Bring water to boil for asparagus spears; salt to taste. Cut off tough bottoms of spears. Scrape sides of each spear and place into boiling water. Cook about 1 minute or until tender-crisp. Drain well. Peel eggs and chop. Heat butter in empty skillet until hot. Add chopped eggs. Cook about 30 seconds. Pour over asparagus.
Makes 4 servings.

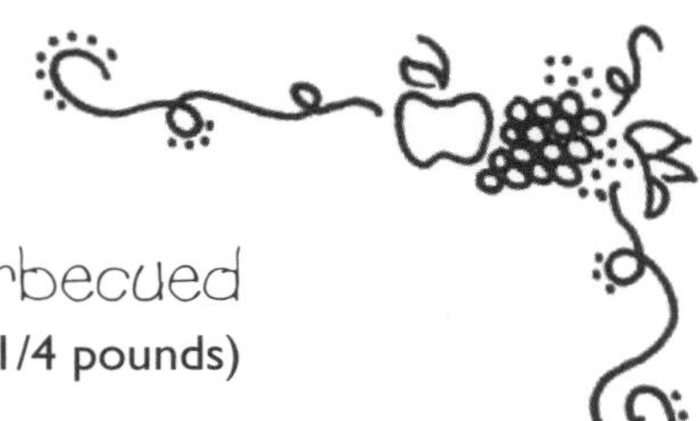

Vegetables Barbecued

4 medium-sized zucchini (about 1-1 1/4 pounds)
4 red, ripe tomatoes
16 large mushrooms (about 3/4 pound total weight)
salt and pepper
1/4 cup olive oil
2 tablespoons basil, chopped

Preheat a charcoal broiler. Trim off ends of zucchini. Split each zucchini in half lengthwise. With sharp paring knife, score the inside of the zucchini. Do not cut the skin.

Arrange on grill, scored side up. Cut around the core of the tomato and remove it. Cut tomato in half, crosswise. Arrange on grill cut side up.

Trim mushrooms - stem level with cap. Sprinkle zucchini, tomatoes and mushrooms with salt and pepper to taste. Brush with garlic oil. Cook 3-4 minutes on each side. Place on platter and sprinkle with basil.

Spinach Souffles

I pound fresh spinach or I 10 ounce package fresh spinach
I/4 cup water
8 eggs, separated
2 tablespoons heavy cream
I/8 teaspoon grated nutmeg
salt and pepper

Butter souffle dishes. Preheat oven to 450 degrees. Pick over spinach removing all tough stems or blemished leaves. Bring water to boil in a 2 quart saucepan. Stir leaves into water until they wilt. Cook about 30 seconds; drain well. Take paper towel and pat out all extra moisture. Put spinach into food processor and make smooth puree. Makes I/2 cup. Put into mixing bowl and add egg yokes, cream and nutmeg; salt and pepper to taste. Beat well.
Beat egg whites until stiff and fold into spinach mixture. Put into souffle dish (about I I/2 cup capacity) and put on cookie sheet. Bake 7 minutes; reduce oven heat to 425 degrees and continue to bake for 5 additional minutes. Makes 4 servings.

Pimientos, Peppers and Potatoes

6-8 potatoes
salt and pepper
3 tablespoons corn oil
1/3 cup onion, finely chopped
1 cup sweet green peppers, diced
1 tablespoon butter
1/3 cup diced pimientos

Peel potatoes. Cut about 1/2 inch thick and cut them into cubes. Put into water in 2 quart saucepan. Bring to boil and simmer 2 minutes. Drain well. Heat oil in a skillet; add potatoes. Shake and stir as necessary until the potatoes are brown (about 8 minutes). Add onion and green peppers. Shake gently about 2 1/2 to 3 minutes. Add butter, cooking 2 minutes longer. Add pimiento and stir gently. Cook until pimientos are heated. Serve immediately. Makes 4 servings.

Buttered Potatoes

1-2 pounds new potatoes (10 small new potatoes)
salt and pepper
3 tablespoons butter

Cook potatoes whole. Drain water. Heat butter in 2 quart skillet. Put whole new potatoes in skillet. Let brown on all sides. Salt and pepper to taste. Makes 4 servings.

My Favorite Vegetables Baked with Mozzarella

1 eggplant
2 zucchini
3 tablespoons olive oil
3/4 cup chopped onions
1 tablespoons garlic, minced
salt and pepper
1 tomato
2 sprigs fresh thyme or 1 teaspoon dried thyme
1 bay leaf
4 slices mozzarella cheese
2 tablespoons grated parmesan cheese

Trim off ends of eggplant and peel. Cut lengthwise into 1 inch slices; cut into cubes. Trim ends of zucchini; cube the same as eggplant. Heat oil in a 2 quart sauce pan; add onions and garlic. Cook about 1/2-1 minute or until onion is wilted. Add eggplant, zucchini and stir. Cook one minute. Add thyme and bay leaf; salt and pepper to taste. Cook 5 minutes; stir as necessary to prevent sticking. Makes 4 servings.

Zucchini-Turnip and Carrots

2 zucchini
2 medium white turnips
2 carrots, trimmed and scraped
salt and pepper
3 tablespoons butter
2 tablespoons shallots, chopped

Cut ends off of zucchini, turnips and carrots. Cut into 1/4 inch slices lengthwise.

Cut carrots into 2 quart saucepan. Cover with water. Salt and pepper to taste. Bring to boil; simmer on medium about 1-2 minutes. Add turnips and simmer 2 minutes. Melt butter in large skillet. Add zucchini, carrots, and turnips along with shallots. Season to taste with salt and pepper. Cook 2-3 minutes on medium. Do not overcook. Serve hot. Check out the sauce section in this book for a mate to go with this one or sprinkle with bacon crumbs. Makes 4 servings.

Corn and Peppers

3 ears of fresh corn
3 large peppers
2 tablespoons butter
1 cup onion, chopped
1 tablespoon hot or mild curry powder
1/2 cup heavy cream
salt and pepper

Clean ears of corn and cut the kernels of corn from cob. Set aside. Core, seed and clean peppers; cut into strips. Heat butter in heavy skillet and add onion. Cook until they wilt. Add pepper strips. Salt and pepper to taste. Cook about 30 seconds. Add curry powder; stir well. Cover and cook over low heat about 5 minutes stirring often. Add corn kernels and stir well. Add cream and cook on medium heat stirring about one minute. Do not overcook. Makes 4 servings.

Frosted Cauliflower

Trim green stems off cauliflower. Boil for 10 minutes or until tender. Put in casserole dish and salt. Pour mustard sauce over cauliflower. Grate 1 cup sharp cheddar cheese on top. Bake for 10 minutes or until cheese melts.

Mustard Sauce

1/2 cup mayonnaise
2 teaspoons prepared mustard

Mix ingredients together.

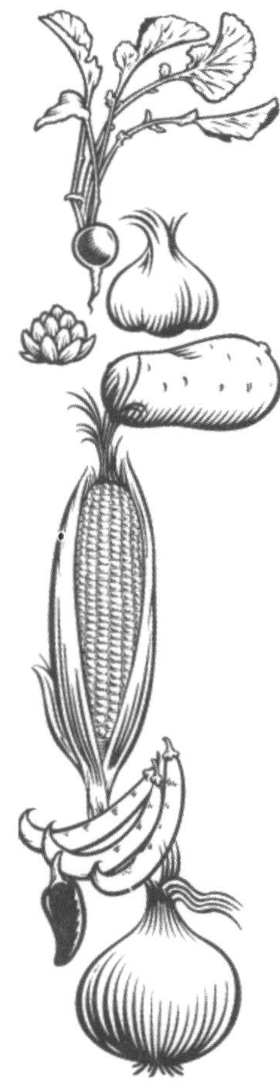

I'll Learn To Eat

Asparagus, peas, okra and squash;
Mom says they're all so yummy.
The thought of eating just one bite
Really hurts my tummy.
When I grow up I'll learn to eat
These veggies "grown ups" call a treat
But until then, Mom, understand,
I'd rather eat the gummies.

Gina Palmer

Fair Game

Thank you, Lord, for my strong teeth
For it is meat I love to eat.
Fried, baked, stewed or grilled,
Anyway is such a thrill.
Gravy, BBQ, or marinade,
With any choice I'll have it made.
Fat, skinny, short or long
They're really all the same
If it has legs to walk around,
Consider it "fair game."

Gina Palmer

Main Courses & Casseroles

A good
meatloaf
is
hard to
beat.
It makes
you want
to eat...
eat...eat!

Shish-Ka-Bob Marinade

2 pounds top round or sirloin, cut into cubes or equivalent of lamb cubes
5/8 cup Crisco oil
1/2 cup soy sauce
1/8 cup Worcestershire sauce
1 tablespoon dry mustard
1 1/8 teaspoon salt
1/2 tablespoon ground pepper
1/8 cup red wine vinegar
5/8 teaspoon dried parsley flakes
1/3 cup fresh lemon juice
1 garlic clove, crushed

In glass bowl, combine all ingredients, except meat. Add meat and marinate the meat overnight, turning whenever possible. Place meat on skewers, alternating pieces of meat with mushrooms, green pepper, tomatoes and pieces of onion. Grill shish-ka-bobs, basting frequently with marinade. Will serve about 4-5 people.

Fried Frog Legs

2-3 pounds frog legs
salt and pepper
2/3 cup milk
1 cup flour
1 cup corn oil

Rinse and pat the legs dry. Cut off and discard bottom of each leg. Place legs into the milk. Dredge each in flour then sprinkle on salt and pepper. Fry in hot oil reduced to medium 4-5 minutes per side. Should be golden brown. Drain on paper towels. Serve immediately.

Happy Crowd Chili

4 pounds ground beef
2 tablespoons olive oil
4 cups onions, chopped
1 1/2 cups green pepper, chopped
3/4 cup celery, chopped
4 bay leaves
2 tablespoons garlic, minced
2 tablespoons oregano
5 tablespoons chili powder
3 cups canned tomatoes
3 cups tomato paste
2 cups beef broth
2 cups water
salt and pepper to taste

Brown the ground beef in skillet. Drain well. Add olive oil; stir. Combine and add all vegetables and spices; stir. In a large pot, bring the tomatoes, paste, and water to a boil. Dump in the ground beef mixture. Reduce heat to low. Allow to simmer for at least an hour to incorporate flavors. Fantastic with shredded cheddar cheese topped with sour cream and a good cake of corn bread. Feeds a large crowd.

Fried Pork Rice

1 pound boneless pork, cut in 3/4 cubes
1-10 ounce can condensed cream of mushroom soup
2 1/4 cups water
2 teaspoons salt
1/2 teaspoon sage
1 cup Uncle Ben's converted rice
1/4 cup pimiento, coursely chopped

Brown pork in cooking oil in large skillet, drain. Stir in soup, water and seasonings. Bring to boil. Cover and cook over low heat 20 minutes. Stir in rice. Cook, covered about 25 minutes or until rice is tender and mixture is desired consistency. Stir occasionally. Stir in pimiento. Makes 4-6 servings.

You may want to add:
1 cup chopped celery with rice
or 1/2 cup green pepper, diced browned with meat
or garnish with chopped parsley before serving. Very good.

from the kitchen of Helen

Beef Stroganoff

1/2 stick margarine
1/2 cup onion, chopped
1 pound ground steak or
 1 pound slivered top
 round steak browned
1 teaspoon salt
1 teaspoon black pepper
1/4 teaspoon paprika
2 tablespoons flour
1 can cream of
 chicken soup
1 small can
 mushrooms, sliced
1 can water
 chestnuts, sliced
1 cup sour cream
dried noodles
cooked rice

Saute onions in margarine. Mix beef, salt, pepper and paprika; add to onion. Cook until meat is grayish color. Blend in flour. Add soup, chestnuts and mushrooms. Cook on low heat for 5 minutes. Add sour cream, remove from heat. Serve on rice with dried noodles on top. Note: stroganoff may be frozen, if desired. Do not boil when reheating.
Yield: 4-6 servings.

from the kitchen of JD

Two Layer Meal

1 pound ground beef
2/3 cup onion, chopped
1 1/2 teaspoon salt
2 tablespoons chili powder
2 medium potatoes,
 peeled and thinly sliced
1/3 cup rice
2/3 cup green bell
 pepper, chopped
1/3 cup catsup
1 no. 2 can tomatoes
1/3 cup water

Place in layers, according to listing, in a casserole dish. Bake covered for 1 hour at 350 degrees.

from the kitchen of JD

Oven Barbecued Chicken

Place frying size pieces of chicken in pan with small amount of water. Cook 1/2 hour on one side. Turn and cook 1/2 hour on other side. Set oven at 350 degrees and prepare sauce as follows:

1 1/2 cups tomato juice
1/4 teaspoon cayenne pepper
2 teaspoons salt
1/4 teaspoon pepper
1/2 teaspoon powdered mustard
5 teaspoons Worcestershire sauce
1 bay leaf
1 teaspoon sugar
3/4 cup cider vinegar
1 medium onion, finely chopped

Mix and simmer 10 minutes. Pour over chicken and continue baking for 20 to 30 minutes.

from the kitchen of JD

Chili for Hot Dogs

1 pound ground beef
1 can tomato soup
1/2 can water
1 tablespoon chili pepper
salt and pepper to taste
catsup to taste

Brown meat (drain off most fat). Add ingredients and simmer. Make paste of 2 tablespoons flour and water to thicken. Simmer a few minutes.

Apple Time Pork Roast

1-5 pound pork roast
1 teaspoon pumpkin pie spice
1 cup apple cider
2 tart cooking apples, peeled, cored and sliced
2 tablespoons brown sugar
2 tablespoons flour
2 tablespoons water
salt and pepper to taste

Brown pork in a large heavy kettle or Dutch oven; remove from heat. Sprinkle meat with pumpkin pie spice and pour cider over the meat. Cover and bake at 325 degrees for 3 hours or until almost tender. Remove meat from kettle. Drain liquid into a 4 cup measure; let stand about one minute, or until fat rises to the top. Skim off the fat. Arrange the sliced apples in the bottom of the kettle. Place the meat on top. Add brown sugar to the drained liquid and stir. Pour over the meat. Bake, uncovered, basting often for 30 minutes or until lightly browned. Remove pork to heated platter. Keep the meat hot while preparing the gravy. In a cup, smooth flour and water to make a paste. Slowly stir into hot liquid in kettle. Place kettle on the top of the stove and cook, on low, stirring constantly and scraping baked on juices from the bottom and sides of the kettle, until gravy thickens and bubbles; about 3 minutes. Add salt and pepper to taste. Slice meat and pass gravy to spoon over.
Serves 6-8

from the kitchen of Lynette Wright

Paillard of Chicken with Apple and Escarole Ragout

from the kitchen of
The Redd Lion, Stockbridge, Massachusetts

3 tablespoons olive oil
1 large white onion, julienned
2 Macoun apples, unpeeled and sliced
3 cups fresh escarole, rinsed and chopped
2 cups apple cider
4 whole boneless chicken breasts, split and lightly pounded
salt and pepper
Dijon Vinaigrette (see recipe below)

Heat 2 tablespoons of the oil in a saute pan and saute the onion until carmelized. Add the apple slices, escarole and cider and cook on high heat until the escarole is wilted and the cider is almost evaporated.

Lightly season the chicken with the salt and black pepper. In another pan, heat the remaining oil and saute the chicken over medium heat for about 3 minutes on each side. Do not overcook.

To assemble, pour one-fourth of the prepared Dijon Vinaigrette on 4 individual plates and place 1/2 cup of the apple/escarole ragout in the center of each plate. Arrange a chicken breast on the mixture and top each with 1/4 cup ragout. Serves 4.

Dijon Vinaigrette

1/2 cup whole grain Dijon mustard
1/4 cup cider vinegar
1/4 cup olive oil

Whisk all of the ingredients together in a small bowl until thoroughly blended. Yield: 1 cup.

Famous Chicken Pie

Cut up 2 medium-sized fat hens and stew until tender; add salt to taste when nearly done. Debone and skin; separate meat into fairly small pieces. Skim fat from top of broth, using some of this, thickened with flour, makes a rich gravy of the broth, adding milk or cream. Season to taste with salt and pepper.

Make this recipe for the crust twice:

- 6 tablespoons flour, heaping
- 4 tablespoons milk
- 2 tablespoons lard, heaping

Add 2 pinches of salt and baking powder to the flour before sifting. Mix the pie dough; roll thin into 2 batches, larger for the bottom crust. Line large, flat cake pan (about 14 1/2 x 9 1/2 inches) with dough. Put chicken in pan next, then completely cover with part of the gravy, reserving the rest to be served with the pie. Add top crust, cutting several slits in it, and place in 400 degree oven, reducing heat when crust begins to brown. Bake about 45 minutes or until golden brown. This will serve from 16-18.

from the kitchen of JD

Gina's Chicken Pot Pie

- 1/3 cup butter or margarine
- 1/2 cup flour
- 1 tablespoon onion flakes
- 1/2 can cream of chicken soup
- 1/2 teaspoon salt
- 1/4 teaspoon pepper
- 2 ready made pie pastries
- 1 3/4 cup water
- 2/3 cup milk
- 2 cups cooked chicken
- 3/4 small can peas
- 3/4 small can carrots

Melt butter over low heat. Stir in flour, onion flakes, soup, salt and pepper until smooth. Add water and milk; stir until boiling. Boil 1 minute. Stir in chicken and vegetables; set aside. Line bottom of pie dish with flour pastry. Pour ingredients in dish. Cover with second flour pastry; cut slots in top to vent. Bake at 425 degrees for 30 minutes.

Easy Lasagna

1 1/2-8 ounce packages wide noodles
salad oil
1 1/2 pounds chuck, ground
1 1/2 teaspoons salt
1/2 teaspoon pepper
2 cups favorite spaghetti sauce
1 pound creamed cottage cheese
1/4 cup sour cream
1 1/2-8 ounce package pizza-cheese slices

Day before or early on day to be used: cook noodles as package label directs; drain, then toss with 2 tablespoons salad oil until well coated. In skillet, brown chuck, then drain very well, add salt, pepper and spaghetti sauce. Stir well. Combine cottage cheese with sour cream.

Arrange half of noodles in 12 x 8 x 2 inch baking dish; cover with half of meat sauce mixture. Add a layer of cheese slices (using 1 package), then all of cottage cheese mixture. Top with remaining noodles, then rest of cheese in 1/2 inch strips, place lattice fashion across top. Then spoon rest of meat sauce mixture into lattice spaces.

Cover tightly with saran or foil, refrigerate.
Heat oven to 350 degrees about 30 minutes before serving. Brush surface of cheese with salad oil. Bake 30 minutes or until cheese melts and is golden. Makes 6 servings. (You may sustitute 1 1/2-8 ounce packages mozzeralla, thinly sliced, for pizza cheese.)

from the kitchen of JD

Baked Apple Pork Chops

6 chops, 3/4 to 1" thick
2 tablespoons lard or drippings
1 1/2 teaspoons salt
1/8 teaspoon pepper
1 jar sliced apple rings
2/3 cup applesauce
1 teaspoon lemon juice
1/3 cup raisins
1 tablespoon cornstarch
1/3 cup water

Brown chops in drippings in oven-proof frying pan or Dutch oven and pour off drippings. Season with salt and pepper. Drain spiced apple rings, reserving liquid. Combine spiced apple liquid, applesauce and lemon juice; add to chops. Stir in raisins, cover and cook in oven at 350 degrees for 1 hour. Remove chops from liquid to hot platter. Combine cornstarch and water to liquid for gravy. Add apple rings to sauce and cook for 1 minute. Arrange chops on hot platter. Serve gravy and apple rings over chops. Makes 6 servings.

from the kitchen of Lynette Wright

Chicken Tetrazzini

1-8 ounce package spaghetti
3 cups cooked chicken, chopped
1/2 pound grated cheese
2 cans mushroom soup
1-8 ounce can mushrooms
1 green pepper, chopped
1 cup celery, chopped
1 onion, chopped

Saute onion, celery and pepper in shortening or oil. Cook spaghetti in 1/2 of chicken stock. Grease casserole. Put half of spaghetti in bottom, then half the chicken, half the mushrooms, half the onion-celery-pepper mixture, half the mushroom soup and half the cheese. Sprinkle with a few spoons of stock, then repeat layers. Top with grated cheese. Bake at 350 degrees for 30 minutes.

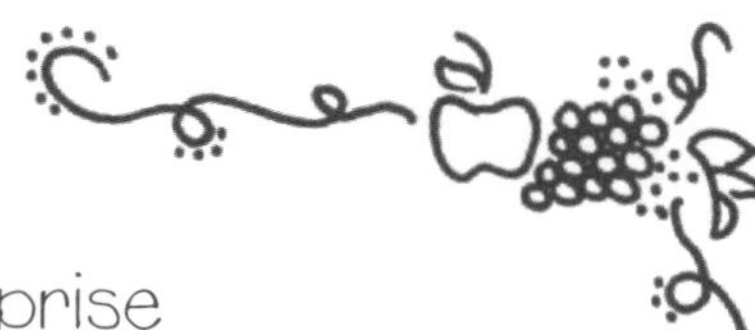

Chicken Surprise

4 chicken breasts
1 bottle of Russian dressing
1 jar of Smucker's Apricot preserves
1 package onion soup mix

Place chicken in a casserole dish with a cover. In a small saucepan, bring dressing and preserves to a boil. Pour over chicken. Sprinkle with onion soup mix. Cover and bake at 350 degrees for 1 hour.

Ham-Broccoli Rolls with Mustard Sauce

8 slices fully cooked, boneless ham, 1/8" thick, about 3/4 pound
1-10 ounce package frozen broccoli spears, cooked and drained
3 tablespoons butter or margarine, melted
2 tablespoons flour
1/4 teaspoon salt
1 cup milk
1/2 cup sour cream
2 tablespoons prepared mustard
1 teaspoon dried chopped chives
4 servings hot fluffy cooked rice, buttered and seasoned

Roll each ham slice around an equal amount of broccoli and arrange in shallow 1 1/2 quart casserole. Brush ham with 1 tablespoon melted butter or margarine. Cover casserole with aluminum foil, crimping it securely to edges. Bake in 400 degree oven for 20 minutes. To prepare sauce while ham rolls are heating, blend remaining 2 tablespoons butter or margarine, flour and salt together in saucepan. Add milk; cook, stirring constantly, until thick and smooth. Stir in sour cream, mustard and chives; heat. Spoon rice over bottom of heated serving dish. Arrange ham rolls on rice and spoon sauce over both. Garnish with watercress, if desired. Makes 4 servings.

from the kitchen of Jane McIntosh

Roasted Beef Fillet

Fillet of beef,
approximately 8-10 inches in length, fat removed
salt and pepper
2 tablespoons corn oil
2 tablespoons butter

Oven should be preheated to 425 degrees. Tie meat into 5 sections, to hold together. Rinse and pat dry. Rub with oil. Place in oven in a shallow roasting pan. Bake for 30 minutes turning twice. Remove from oven and pour off fat. Add butter and return to oven and continue baking for 10 minutes, turning once. Remove from oven and cut away strings. Slice and place on plate; pour pan drippings over meat and seal with aluminum foil until ready to serve. For more rare meat, reduce baking time by 5 minutes and serve at once.

Party Beef Fondue

3 pounds sirloin steak, cut into 1"x1" cubes
romain lettuce and watercress
Dijon mustard
peanut oil
sauces for dipping

Arrange cubed steak on a bed of the mixed lettuce. Pour sauces into individual serving bowls. Heat oil in saucepan on top of stove until very hot. Transfer to metal fondue pot. Place fondue pot on stand over the burner. Each guest cooks their own steak. Makes 6-8 servings. Serve with raw vegetables, if desired.

Rattle Snake

1 rattlesnake, skinned and cleaned (watch the teeth!)
2 eggs
flour
salt
pepper
1 cup white wine
1/2 stick butter/oleo

Cut meat in sections, dip in egg and flour, then saute in butter over low heat 10 minutes per side. Season with salt and pepper. Add wine and cook 10 to 15 minutes more! Cut into bite-sized pieces. Serve on toothpicks.

There's
nothing in
life
better than
a day
spent
fishing.
Paul Newman, Jr.

Seafood

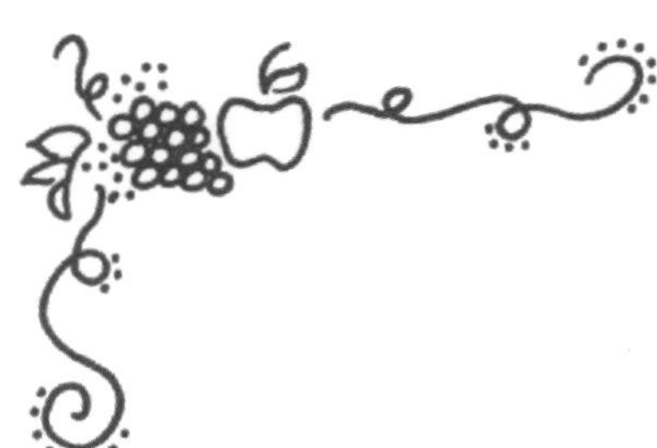

seafood

Catch of the Day with Vegetables

1 3/4 skinless, boneless fish
1/4 cup olive oil
1 cup onions, chopped
2 cups sweet green or red peppers, chopped
2 cloves garlic, peeled and minced
1 1/4 cup leeks, chopped
1 dried hot red pepper
1 bay leaf
1/2 teaspoon dried thyme
salt and pepper
2 cups tomatoes, peeled and cubed
1 cup dry wine
1 cup potatoes, peeled and cubed
3 cups fish broth (can cook head of fish)
1/2 cup heavy cream
1/4 cup parsley, chopped

Cut fish into 1-inch cubes. Set aside. Heat oil in skillet; add onions. Cook until wilted. Add pepper, garlic, leeks and cook, stirring about one minute. Add hot red pepper, bay leaf and thyme; salt and pepper to taste. Cook about 4-5 minutes. Add tomatoes and cook stirring about one minute. Add wine and potatoes and cover. Cook 10 minutes. Add fish broth and fish. Cook 5 minutes. Add cream and bring to a boil; serve hot. Sprinkle with parsley.

This is a good recipe with french bread. Makes 4 servings.

Sole Madras

curry powder
4 tablespoons coriander
3 tablespoons cumin
3 tablespoons turmeric
3 tablespoons cardamon
1 teaspoon mace
1 teaspoon cinnamon
1 teaspoon cloves
1/2 teaspoon or less cayenne

Grind finely all the ingredients, put in glass jar and shake well. Mix 1/3 curry powder and 2/3 flour. Season sole fillets with salt and lemon juice. Let marinade for 10-15 minutes. Dry lightly, then dip in flour curry mix in large skillet with thin layer of sesame seed oil. Heat to almost smoking. Lay in fish and 1/2 banana, which you first dip in the curry flour mix also. Brown, turn and brown. Arrange on plate. Brown a teaspoon of chopped almonds, then add freshly chopped pineapple. Saute until all juice is reduced. Add a tablespoon of lemon juice and a teaspoon of chopped parsley or salentro. Put topping of fish and decorate with fresh fruit such as mango, papaya, kiwis, peaches or berries. Serve mango chutney and fresh cucumber or tomato.

Relish:
1 medium tomato, chunked
1/2 cucumber, chunked
1/4 medium onion, chunked
Add 1 tablespoon parsley, chopped
1 tablespoon vinegar
salt to taste

from the kitchen of Donna Durgin

Captain Sam's Tugboat Mull

2 pounds medium shrimp
1 quart oysters
1 can crab soup
seasonings to taste
8 cups minute rice
1/2 pound lean bacon
1 large onion, finely chopped
1/2 stalk celery, finely chopped
1 medium green pepper, finely chopped
1 pound red snapper fillets
seasoned cracker crumbs

Peel, devein and wash shrimp. Place in seasoned boiling water; cook until done. Drain and reserve stock. Set shrimp aside. Check oysters for any shell; drain in colander, reserving juice. Rinse; place in saucepan. Add reserved oyster juice and small amount of water.
Cook until edges curl. Drain and reserve juice. Set oyster aside. Combine soup, one soup can of water, reserved stock from shrimp and oysters in saucepan; bring to a boil. Remove from heat; measure and place in a 1 gallon kettle. Add enough water to make 10 cups. Remove 2 cups of this broth and save in reserve; season the broth to taste. Bring to a slow boil. Add rice; stir once. Cover; let stand for 20 minutes. Cut bacon crosswise into 1/4 inch pieces. Place bacon, onion, celery and green pepper in skillet; fry until bacon is done but not crisp. Drain off drippings and reserve. Set bacon mixture aside. Cut the snapper into 3-inch long, 3/4-inch wide and 1/2-inch thick strips. Coat with crumbs. Place in greased baking pan. Bake in preheated 350 degree oven for 15 minutes. Remove from oven and cool. Add bacon mixture to rice; stir to mix well. Grease a 9 1/2 x 13 1/2 x 1 1/2 inch pan with reserved bacon drippings. Place 1/2 inch layer of rice mixture in pan. Cover rice with oysters; add a 1 inch layer of rice. Cover with layer of shrimp, then add remaining rice. Place snapper over rice; press down lightly. Pour 2 cups reserved broth over top. Bake in oven preheated to 350 degrees for 10 minutes or until heated through. Garnish with paprika and parsley before serving. May boil snapper bones for the 2 cups broth and add only enough water to make 8 cups before adding rice, if desired.

from the kitchen of Sam A. Jessup

Mushrooms and Scallops in Cream Sauce

3 tablespoons butter
2 tablespoons shallots, chopped
1/4 pound mushrooms, sliced thick
1 tablespoons lemon juice
1 pound scallops
salt and pepper to taste
2 tablespoons cognac
1 cup heavy cream

Heat 2 tablespoons of butter in a skillet (2 quart size). Put scallops in skillet. Must have room to sear; add shallots. Cook about 30 seconds, stirring. Add mushrooms and half of lemon juice. Cook about 1 minute. Add scallops; salt and pepper to taste. Cook over high heat, shaking skillet about 1 1/2 minutes; sprinkle with cognac. Ignite. Cook briefly. Transfer scallops and mushrooms to a bowl to collect juice. Put the cream and any juice that have accumulated from scallops into skillet. Cook down over high heat, stirring 2 minutes. The sauce should be reduced to 1 cup. Add remaining lemon juice and swirl in remaining butter. Add scallops and mushrooms to the cream sauce and reheat briefly. Serve hot over rice. Yields: 4 servings.

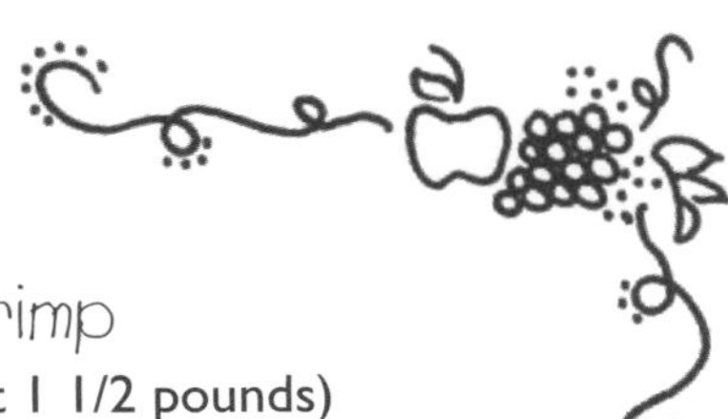

Stuffed Shrimp

25-30 medium to large shrimp (about 1 1/2 pounds)
5 tablespoons butter
1/2 cup onions, chopped
1 cup mushrooms, chopped
1/2 cup celery
1/2 teaspoon garlic, minced
salt and pepper
3/4 cup bread crumbs
1/4 cup parsley
1 egg, lightly beaten

Peel and devein shrimp. Preheat oven broiler. Set aside 23-25 shrimp. Chop the remaining shrimp coarsely. Heat 2 tablespoons butter in saucepan. Add onion, celery and garlic. Cook until wilted; stir in mushrooms; salt and pepper to taste. Cook for 3 minutes.

Remove from heat. Mix in the chopped shrimp. Add bread crumbs, parsley and egg. Mix well. Salt to taste. Butterfly shrimp by slicing them down the back. Spoon stuffing on top of shrimp. Grease a baking dish or cookie sheet with butter. Arrange shrimp single layer in baking dish or on cookie sheet. Place sheet or dish on stovetop to bring juices around shrimp (butter will melt). Place under broiler for 5 minutes until shrimp are nicely browned.

Bar-B-Q-Tuna

1-6 1/2 ounce tuna, drained
1 tablespoon Worcestershire sauce
2 teaspoons onion flakes
2 teaspoons wine vinegar
chili powder to taste
1 teaspoon prepared mustard
1/2 cup V-8 or tomato juice

Mix all together. Simmer until hot.

Tuna and Biscuit Roll

3/4 cup grated cheese
1 small can tuna, drained
2 tablespoons onion, chopped
rich White Sauce
biscuit dough

White Sauce:
2 tablespoons oleo
2 tablespoons onion
1/2 cup milk
3/4 cup grated cheese

Cook onions in oleo on medium heat until lightly brown. Add milk, tuna and 3/4 cup cheese. Cook until boiling. Drain and set aside. Flatten out biscuit dough and add mixture to center. Add cheese to the top. Roll biscuit over until all mixture is covered. Bake in 350 degree oven until dough is browned.

Deviled Crab

4 tablespoons butter or margarine
1 tablespoon parsley, chopped
1 teaspoon prepared mustard
1 teaspoon salt
2 cups crab meat
1/2 cup buttered bread crumbs
2 tablespoons flour
2 teaspoons lemon juice
1/2 teaspoon horseradish
1 cup milk
2 hard-boiled eggs

Mix butter and flour in saucepan over medium heat. Stir until smooth. Add all remaining ingredients. Mix well and put into crab shells. Sprinkle with buttered crumbs. Bake for 10 minutes at 400 degrees. Serves 6.

Crispy Fried Fish

2 eggs
1/4 cup prepared mustard
1/2 teaspoon seafood seasoning
1 1/2 pounds fish fillets
instant mashed potato flakes
oil or melted shortening

Beat together eggs, mustard, parsley and seafood seasoning. Dip fish in the mustard mixture; roll in potato flakes. Fry in hot oil or shortening 3 to 4 minutes on each side until golden brown. Serves 4.

You can also "oven fry fish." Heat the oven to 350 degrees. Put a tablespoon of oil in nonstick pan. Place prepared fish fillets in pan. Cook in oven until fish is brown and flakes easily when tested with a fork.

Sizzled Oysters

2-4 tablespoons butter
garlic salt to taste
onion salt to taste
pepper or lemon pepper
1 pint oysters

Sizzle oysters in butter until edges curl in heavy skillet; add seasoning and transfer to heated chafing dish. Serve with toothpicks, Triscuits or saltines. Cocktail sauce is nice also.

Crab Gumbo

1/2 cup celery, chopped
1/2 cup onion, chopped
1 clove garlic, chopped
1/4 pound butter
1/2 pound crabmeat
10 ounces okra, diced
2 1/2 cans whole tomatoes
1/2 teaspoon crushed thyme
1/4 teaspoon sugar
2 teaspoons salt
black pepper to taste
1 bay leaf
1/2 pound cooked crab claws

In a large kettle, saute celery, onion and garlic in butter; add crabmeat and cook until tender. Add okra, tomatoes and seasoning. Simmer, covered for 45 minutes. Remove bay leaf. Add crab claws and simmer, uncovered, for another 10 minutes. Serves 4.

Stuffed Lobster

4 live lobsters
7 tablespoons butter
2 tablespoons shallots, chopped
1/4 cup onion, chopped
1/4 cup loosely packed fresh basil, chopped
or 2 teaspoons dried basil
1/2 teaspoon garlic, minced
salt and pepper
1 1/2 cups soft bread crumbs
1/4 cup vegetable oil

Preheat oven to 450 degrees by broiler. Insert knife into lobster where tail and body meets to sever spinal cord. Pull off claws, crack them and set aside. Cut lobster in half lengthwise. Discard the small sac near eyes and the intestinal tract. Arrange lobster halves, split side up in baking dish. Arrange claws in second baking dish.
Melt one tablespoon of butter in saucepan. Add shallots, onion and garlic. Cook stirring until wilted. Cool. Add bread crumbs to shallot mixture; add remaining butter and basil; salt and pepper to taste. Blend with fingers.
Stuff the cavities of lobster halves. Dribble oil over top. Place baking dish under broiler about 4 inches away. Broil lobster claws and halves 7-8 minutes. Turn off broiler and bake lobster halves 15 minutes and the claws 20 minutes. Serve with butter sauce. Servings: 4.

Sprinkle a handful of coffee over fish in your refrigerator and there will be no noticeable odor.

Avocado and Tequila Shrimp

1 pound shrimp
1/4 cup lime juice
salt and pepper
1 ripe avocado
2 tablespoons butter
1 tablespoon shallot, chopped
1/4 cup tequila
3/4 heavy cream

Shell, devein and butterfly shrimp. Place in bowl. Add lime juice. Let stand until ready to cook.
Peel avocado and cut into 1/2-inch thick slices. Discard seeds. Heat butter in skillet and add shrimp. When hot, cook 2 minutes stirring rapidly. Sprinkle shallots and cook stirring 10 seconds. Add tequila. Add cream and cook over high heat about 1 minutes. Add salt and pepper to taste. Fold in avocado and cook until slices are hot. Do not overcook. Put on hot serving dish and bring sauce to a rolling boil. Pour over shrimp. Servings: 4.

Hot Salmon Mousses

1 pound boneless, skinless salmon fillet
2 egg whites
5 drops of tabasco sauce
salt and pepper
2 teaspoons fresh dill, chopped
1 cup heavy cream
fresh dill sprigs

Dice salmon. Place in food processor until fine. Add egg whites and Tabasco sauce; salt and pepper to taste.
Add the chopped dill and cream. Process until combined. Butter baking mold dish. Spoon in salmon mixture. Put molds in saucepan and pour hot water to come to rim of molds. Cover the saucepan and simmer gently - low heat for 15 minutes or until mousse is set and firm. Unmold onto a warmed serving dish. Garnish with dill sprigs. Can be served with hollandaise sauce. Servings: 4-6.

Fish Soup

1/2 pound potatoes
1 1/2 pounds of fish fillets or Cod fish
3 1/2 tablespoons olive oil
1/2 cup onions, chopped
1 teaspoon garlic, chopped
1/2 cup leeks, chopped
1/2 cup carrots
1 dried hot red pepper
1 bay leaf
2 teaspoons fresh thyme, chopped or
 1/2 teaspoon dried thyme
1 cup dry white wine
1 cup tomatoes, chopped
1 cup water
1/2 pound scallops
1 cup heavy cream
1/4 cup parsley
salt and pepper

Peel and cube potatoes. Place into cold water. Cut fish into cubes; set aside. Heat oil in skillet and add onion, garlic, green pepper, leeks and carrots. Cook stirring often until onion wilts. Add red pepper, bay leaf, thyme, wine and tomatoes. Bring to a boil. Drain cold water from potatoes and add them to mixture; cover and cook 10 minutes adding one cup of water. Cook uncovered 5 minutes. Add fish and scallops; cook 2-3 minutes. Do not overcook. Add cream and bring to boil. Gently stir in parsley. Salt and pepper to taste. Serve piping hot. French bread is good with this dish. Servings: 4.

Grits and Cheese

1 1/2 cups white grits
6 cups water (do not add salt to water)
3 beaten eggs
1 stick unsalted butter
1/2 pound grated longhorn cheese
1/2 pound grated sharp cheddar cheese
1 teaspoon seasoning salt
dash of Tabasco
dash of paprika

Prepare eggs, butter and cheeses and have ready for quick combining.
Bring water to boil and add grits slowly - cook until done. Add salt and Tabasco. Immediately add eggs, longhorn and cheddar cheeses to the hot grits. Stir until the eggs, butter and cheeses are well combined. Pour mixture into a large baking dish (pre-buttered). Sprinkle with paprika. Bake at 250 degrees 1 to 1 1/2 hours depending on depth of baking dish or until lightly brown and puffy all over top. Serves: 12. Good with fish.

from the kitchen of George

Shrimp with Mayo Sauce

1 1/2 pounds shrimp, cooked, shelled and deveined
1 egg yolk
1 teaspoon mustard
2 teaspoons vinegar
salt and pepper
1 cup peanut oil
1 tablespoon capers, chopped
3 tablespoons sour pickles, chopped
2 tablespoons fresh parsley, chopped
2 teaspoons fresh tarragon, chopped or
  1/2 teaspoon dried tarragon
juice of 1/2 lemon
8 leaves of Boston lettuce
2 hard-boiled eggs, peeled and quartered
8 cherry tomatoes

Leave shrimp whole or if shrimp is large cut them in halves. Set aside.

Combine egg yolks and add mustard, vinegar, salt and pepper. Start beating with wire whisk. Add oil beating vigorously with whisk.

Squeeze capers in paper towel to take away excess liquid. Add capers to mayo. Add parsley and tarragon. Blend well. Put shrimp in bowl and sprinkle lemon juice over them. Add mayo sauce and fold together. Arrange lettuce leaves on 4 plates. Spoon equal amounts of shrimp mixture onto lettuce. Garnish with eggs and tomatoes. Servings: 4.

Oysters and Scallops in Cream Sauce

6 tablespoons butter
2 tablespoons shallots
1/2 cup dry white wine
1 pint bay scallops
1/2 pint shucked oysters with some natural liquid
1/2 cup heavy cream
salt and pepper
2 tablespoons fresh parsley, chopped

Melt 2 tablespoons of butter in a flameproof casserole and add shallots. Cook briefly, stirring. Add wine; cook until wine has almost evaporated. Add scallops and oysters. Cook stirring occasionally about 1 1/2 to 2 minutes. Add the cream and any additional liquid from scallops and oysters. Salt and pepper to taste. Cook over high heat about 2 minutes. Cut remaining butter into pieces; add one piece at a time to sauce. Stir. Fold in parsley, scallops and oysters. Servings: 4.

Crabmeat on English Muffins

1 stick softened oleo
1 jar Old English cheese spread
1 1/2 teaspoons mayonnaise
1/4 teaspoon garlic salt
1/4 teaspoon seasoned salt
1-7 ounce can crabmeat, flaked
6 English muffins

Soften butter and mix all ingredients together except for crabmeat. Drain the crab before adding to mixture. Spread on each muffin half and bake 8 to 10 minutes in a 350 degree oven. Cut into fourths. Makes 48 pieces.

Stuffed Buns

1/4 pound cheese, cubed
3 hard-cooked eggs, chopped
1-7 ounce can flaked tuna
2 tablespoons green pepper, chopped
2 tablespoons onion, chopped
2 tablespoons sweet pickle, chopped
1/2 cup mayonnaise or salad dressing
6-8 hot dog rolls

Combine ingredients. Mix lightly. Split buns (take out a little of bun filling) and fill with mixture. Wrap each bun in foil. Place in low oven about 30 minutes until filling is heated and cheese melts. Serve hot. Fills 6 buns generously.

Clam Chowder

1 dozen clams, in their shells
2 tablespoons bacon drippings
4 medium potatoes, peeled and diced
3 onions, diced
4 stalks celery, diced
1 large can of whole tomatoes
1 tablespoon sugar
pepper to taste

Place the clams and 4 cups of water in a large saucepan. Cover; cook over high heat for 10 minutes, or until the clams have opened. Drain, reserving the liquid. Remove the clams from their shells, discarding the shells, and grind with a meat grinder. Set aside.

Heat the bacon drippings in a kettle over medium heat. Add the potatoes, onion, celery, tomatoes, sugar and the reserved clam liquid. Stew for about 40 minutes or until the vegetables are soft.

Add the clams and season with freshly ground pepper to taste. Simmer over low heat for 15 to 20 more minutes. Serve with crackers or toast. Yield: 4-6 servings.

Deviled Crab Casserole

1 pound crabmeat, preferably lump,
picked over to remove any remaining shell
1 cup saltine crumbs
1 large stalk celery, finely diced
1 hard-boiled egg, finely diced
1 egg
1 cup mayonnaise
2 tablespoons prepared mustard
1 tablespoon Worcestershire sauce
lemon wedges for garnish

Preheat oven to 375 degrees. Mix all ingredients together, making sure the saltines are blended in well. If the mixture is stiff, add a little more mayonnaise. Pack into a decorative baking dish.

Bake for 30 to 35 minutes, until top is golden brown. Serve with lemon wedges on the side. Yield: 4-6 servings.

Breads

The smell of fresh *baking* is sweeter than any perfume.

Sunlight and Shadows

As the sun sets over my garden
And shadows the far away hills
Each day I see seems like the first time
And my heart is gladdened and thrilled
To know such beauty can't be equaled
By any mortals hand
The mighty power I feel there
In awe, I can't help but stand
The hope and inspiration you give me
Are blessings truly indeed
You always know my every thought
And anticipate my every need.
So, Lord, as I stand in awe in my garden
And the sun slowly fades away
Humbly I come before you,
Hoping I've pleased you this day.

Sharon Strickland

Croutons

I loaf Italian bread (at least one day old)
equal parts of butter and oil for frying

Slice bread in I" slices. Stack slices 3-4 on top of each other and slice down the middle, then, turn bread 1/2 turn and slice again. Should be four equal parts (may cut into smaller croutons, if desired). We make ours large to be eaten like saltines or either to top the soups or salads.

Heat oil and butter until hot. Place croutons a few at a time, in pan. Turn with spatula quickly as not to burn. Fry until equally golden brown. Drain on paper towels.

Peach Bread

3 cups peaches, chopped
3 tablespoons orange juice
2/3 cup honey
1/3 cup butter or margarine
2 eggs, beaten
2 cups whole wheat pastry flour
1 cup soy flour
1 teaspoon baking powder
2/3 cup oats
1/2 cup walnuts or pecans
1/2 teaspoon baking soda

Puree 1 cup of peaches in the blender with the orange juice, set aside. In a large bowl, cream together the honey and butter, stir in the eggs and peach puree. In another bowl, mix flours, baking powder, baking soda, oats and nuts. Add to the liquid mixture and the 2 remaining cups of chopped peaches. Bake in a greased 9 x 5 inch bread pan, for about 75 minutes.

Chocolate Orange Bread

3 cups all purpose flour
1 cup sugar
4 teaspoons baking powder
1 1/2 teaspoon salt
1 teaspoon ground cinnamon
1 teaspoon nutmeg
1/2 cup nuts, chopped
2 tablespoons salad oil
3 tablespoons orange rind, grated
1-6 ounce package semi-sweet chocolate chips
1 egg
1 1/4 cup orange juice

Combine flour, sugar, baking powder, salt and spices in large bowl. Stir in nuts, orange rind and chocolate chips. Beat egg in small bowl; beat in orange juice and salad oil. Add to flour mixture; mix well. Pour into greased 9 x 5 x 3 inch loaf pan. Bake at 300 degrees for 1 hour and 15 minutes, or until done. Cool. Drizzle glaze over top.

Orange Glaze:

2 cups powdered sugar
2-4 tablespoons orange juice

Combine and mix until smooth and creamy.

Meaty and Hot Cornbread

1 cup plus 1 tablespoon yellow cornmeal, divided
1 cup milk
2 eggs
3/4 teaspoon salt
1 1/2 teaspoons soda
1/2 cup bacon drippings
1-17 ounce can cream-style corn
1 1/2 pounds ground beef
1 large onion, chopped
1-8 ounce package cheddar cheese, shredded
4 jalapeno peppers, finely chopped

Combine 1 cup cornmeal, milk, eggs, salt, soda, bacon drippings and corn in a bowl; mix and set aside. Saute ground beef until lightly browned; drain thoroughly and set aside. Sprinkle remaining cornmeal in a greased 10 1/2 inch iron skillet; pour half of cornmeal batter in skillet. Sprinkle evenly with beef; top with onions, then cheese. Add peppers evenly on top. Pour remaining batter over top. Bake at 350 degrees for 50 minutes or until golden brown. Servings: 6-8.

Bread Sticks

1 king-size loaf bread
1 cup bread crumbs (made from crust)
1 cup peanut butter
1/3 cup Wesson oil
3/4 cup sesame seed

Trim crust from bread. Cut bread into strips. Bake strips and crusts 1 hour in 250 degree oven. Crumble crusts. Heat oil and peanut butter over low heat, stirring to mix well. Dip bread strips into oil mixture. Roll in crumbs and sesame seed.

Pumpkin Bread

2 eggs, beaten
1 1/2 cups sugar
1/3 cup oil
1 cup pumpkin
1 2/3 cups plain flour
3/4 teaspoon salt
1/2 teaspoon cloves
1 teaspoon nutmeg
1 teaspoon cinnamon (optional)
1/3 cup nuts
1 teaspoon soda dissolved in 1/3 cup cold water

Mix all ingredients together. Grease and flour (2) loaf pans. Bake at 325 degrees for 1 hour.

Beer Bread

3 cups self-rising flour
3 tablespoons sugar
1 can beer (not light)
1/2 stick margarine, melted

Combine flour, sugar and beer; mix well. Turn into well-greased loaf pan. Brush top with melted margarine. Bake at 350 degrees for 1 hour.
Variation: form into rolls, adjusting cooking time.

Honey Cornmeal Biscuits

1 3/4 cups Bisquick
1/2 cup yellow cornmeal
1/2 cup milk
2 tablespoons honey

Honey Butter:
1/2 cup butter
1/4 cup honey
1/2 teaspoon orange zest

Mix all ingredients to form dough. Turn dough on floured surface. Knead 8 to 10 times. Roll out to 1/2 inch thick. Cut with 2 inch cutter. Place in ungreased cookie sheet. Bake at 400 degrees for 8 to 10 minutes or until golden brown. Honey Butter: Beat all together until fluffy. Serve on biscuits.

Slow Cooker Cabbage Rolls

12 large cabbage leaves
1 cup cooked rice
1 beaten egg
1/4 cup milk
1/4 cup onion, finely chopped
1 teaspoon salt
1/4 teaspoon pepper
1 pound lean ground beef
1-8 ounce tomato sauce
1/4 cup water
1 tablespoon brown sugar
1 tablespoon lemon juice
1 teaspoon Worcestershire sauce

Immerse cabbage leaves in boiling water about 3 minutes until limp, drain. Place about 1/4 cup mixture of rice, egg, milk, onion, salt, pepper and ground beef in center of each leaf. Fold in sides and roll ends over meat. Place in pot. Combine rest of ingredients and pour over cabbage rolls. Cover and cook on low 7 to 9 hours. Makes 6 servings.

Yeast Bread

Scald 2 cups milk. Pour over 2 heaping tablespoons shortening, 1/4 cup sugar, 1/2 tablespoon salt. Let cool. Thicken with 2 cups flour. Beat well. Add package of yeast which has begun to rise in 1/2 cup warm water and 1/2 teaspoon sugar. Beat well. Add flour (3 or more cups) to make dough firm. Knead until smooth. Let rise in warm place until twice its bulk. Work and divide into two loaves. Shape and put in greased pans. Let rise 15-20 minutes.

Bake at 375 degrees until bread begins to brown. Place shallow pan of water over the rack and bake at 300 degrees for 20 more minutes.

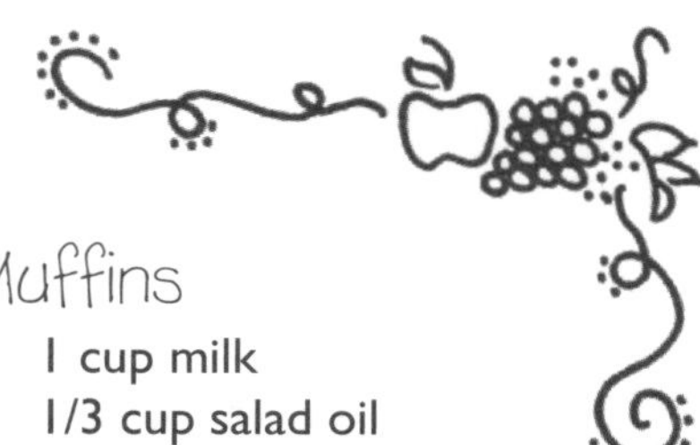

Marvelous Muffins

2 cups sifted flour
1/4 cup sugar
3 teaspoons baking powder
1/2 teaspoon salt
1 cup milk
1/3 cup salad oil
1 egg

Preheat oven to 400 degrees. Grease bottom of 14 (1/2") muffin pan cups or 11 (3").
Sift flour with sugar, baking powder, and salt into large bowl. Measure milk in a 2 cup measure. Add oil and egg; beat with fork to mix well. Make a well in center of flour mixture. Pour in milk mixture all at once; stir quickly with fork, just until flour disappears. Do not beat. The batter will be lumpy. Dip batter into muffin cups and bake 20 to 25 minutes. Bacon Muffins: Add 1/2 cup coarsely chopped, crisp-cooked bacon to dry ingredients. Reduce salad oil to 1/4 cup.

Poppy Seed Pound Cake Muffins

2 cups flour
3 teaspoons poppy seed
1/2 teaspoon salt
1/4 teaspoon soda
1 cup sugar
1/2 cup butter
2 eggs
1 cup plain yogurt
1 teaspoon vanilla

In small bowl stir flour, poppy seed, salt and soda. In large bowl, cream sugar and butter. Beat in eggs, one at a time. Beat in yogurt and vanilla until well blended. Stir in flour mixture until moistened thoroughly. Grease muffin tins. Bake at 400 degrees for 15 to 20 minutes.

Popovers

Place 1 cup milk, 1/2 teaspoon salt and 1/4 cup butter or margarine into a saucepan and bring to a boil, stirring.

Add 1 cup stirred WW flour all at once. Stir vigorously until the dough forms a ball and follows the spoon around the pan. Cool slightly. (I usually put it in a mixing bowl, which helps to cool it.)

Add 3 eggs, one at a time, beating each egg in well.

Divide into 12 greased muffin cups. The dough will still be warm.

Bake at 400 degrees for 35 to 40 minutes. Do not open the oven until the last 5 minutes of baking.

Note: These popovers may be reheated, uncovered, on a cookie sheet at 350 degrees.

Squash Muffins

2 cups flour
1 cup milk
1/2 cup sugar
1/2 teaspoon salt
1 egg
2/3 cup grated squash
1 tablespoon baking powder
2 tablespoons oil

Beat egg. Add milk and squash. Add dry ingredients and oil. Bake at 400 degrees for 18-20 minutes.

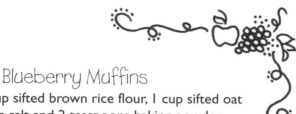

Blueberry Muffins

Mix together 1 cup sifted brown rice flour, 1 cup sifted oat flour, 1/2 teaspoon salt and 2 teaspoons baking powder. Beat together 2/3 cup milk, 2 eggs, 1/4 cup oil and 2 tablespoons brown sugar or honey.

Make a well in the dry ingredients and add liquid all at once. Stir until just moistened.

Fold in 1 cup well-drained canned blueberries and 1 tablespoon blueberry juice.

Fill 12 greased muffin cups. Bake at 400 degrees for about 25 minutes.

Note: These muffins can be frozen, then reheated on an uncovered cookie sheet at 350 degrees for 15 to 20 minutes.

Zucchini Nut Muffins

3 eggs
1 cup oil
1 tablespoon vanilla
2 cups zucchini, unpeeled and shredded
1 cup brown sugar
1 cup granulated white sugar
2 cups plain flour
1 tablespoon cinnamon
1 1/2 teaspoon baking soda
1 teaspoon salt
1/4 teaspoon baking powder
1 cup chopped pecans

Combine eggs, oil, vanilla and zucchini. Add remaining ingredients and stir. Heat oven to 400 degrees. Grease and flour muffin tins. Fill 2/3 full. Bake 18 minutes.

Sour Cream Bread

Beat together 3 tablespoons oil and 2 tablespoons honey. Add 3 eggs and beat well.

Mix together 1 cup sifted brown rice flour, 1 cup oat flour, 1 1/4 teaspoon salt, 2 teaspoons baking powder and 1/4 teaspoon soda.

Add half of the flour mixture to the egg mixture, blending well. Add 1 cup sour cream, then the rest of the flour. Mix well.

Pour into greased and floured bundt pan or glass loaf pan.
Bake at 350 degrees for 40 to 45 minutes.

Allow to cool in pan for 5 minutes. Remove to rack to finish cooling.

Spicy Raisin Bread

Make Sour Cream Bread recipe and add 2 teaspoons cinnamon, 1/4 teaspoon nutmeg, and 1 cup raisins to the flour mixture.

Quick Rye Bread

Make Sour Cream Bread recipe but use 2/3 cup each of sifted brown rice, oat and rye flours instead of the 1 cup each of rice and oat flours. Also, add 1 tablespoon caraway seeds.

Golden Heart Bread

2 packages yeast
1/4 cup lukewarm water
2 cups boiling water
5 cups nonfat dry milk
2 tablespoons solid shortening
2 tablespoons sugar
2 teaspoons salt
5 cups flour
2 1/2 cups wheat germ (raw)

Mix yeast with lukewarm water and set aside. Mix boiling water and dry milk together with electric mixer, then add rest of ingredients (solid shortening through salt). Cool to lukewarm. Add yeast and half of flour, stirring well. Add wheat germ and rest of flour to form soft dough; let rest 10 minutes. Knead (this is a very sticky dough, knead with oiled hands). Shape into 2 balls, cover and rest for 10 minutes. Place in bread pans. Let rise until doubled, about 90 minutes. Bake at 350 degrees for 40 to 50 minutes.

Buttermilk Biscuits

2 cups self-rising flour
1/2 cup Wesson oil
1 cup buttermilk
pinch of baking soda

Mix together with hands. Mold into small balls and roll in flour. Place on lightly greased cookie sheet and slightly flatten balls of dough. Bake at 375 degrees until golden brown on top.

Our
taste
buds
are
more
demanding
than our
conscience.

Cookies & Candy

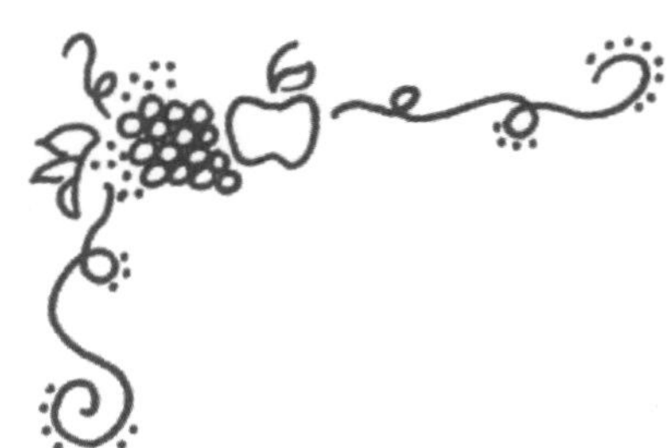

cookies & candy

Leaving One Book Signing, Getting Ready For Another...

Dear Lord,

I thank you for the beauty you've allowed me to see;
And every place you land me is just where I want to be.
I thank you for allowing me to be completely diversified,
With the absolute knowledge that you're always by my side.
Once more, dear Lord, I ask your favor;
Help my faith grow strong and never waiver.
Remind me, dear Jesus, to ever be grateful;
Open my eyes when I'm mean and hateful.

Amen,
Sharon Strickland

How sweet it is...

A Riddle Recipe

Old Mother Goose baked some cookies one day;
She filled up her jar and then hid it away
In Mother Hubbard's cupboard so big and bare;
Thinking that no one would find it there.
But the Nursery Rhyme people, at a party that night,
Discovered the goodies and ate every bite!

When Old Mother Goose went to the cupboard the next day to get some cookies, she found they were all gone, and began to cry. The Nursery Rhyme people felt ashamed because they had eaten all her cookies. So they decided to help her make some more. Each one gave her something to put in them and helped her bake them. All poor Mother Goose had was a little soda, baking powder and salt. See if you can guess what the Nursery Rhyme people gave to put in the cookies, which were very good. Then, see below for the right answers.

1. 1/4 cup of what Jack Sprat could not eat.
2. 1 cup of the first thing that little girls are made of.
3. 3/4 teaspoon of the second thing little girls are made of.
4. Humpty Dumpty
5. 2 cups of what the little hen went to the mill to fetch.
6. 1/2 cup of what Little Miss Muffet was eating.
7. Mix these in what the Three Wise Men went to sea in.
8. Stir them with what the Dish ran away with.

You, yourself can make these good cookies by following the recipe carefully, after filling in the right answers; cream number 1 and number 2 together until smooth and light. Beat number 4 and stir it in. Sift number 5 with 1/2 teaspoon salt, 1/4 teaspoon soda and 1 teaspoon baking powder. Add this and number 6 a little at a time, to the creamed mixture. Add number 3 and mix in 1/2 cup of raisins and 1/2 cup nuts. Drop by teaspoonfuls on a greased baking sheet. Bake in a hot oven, 400 degrees, for about 15 minutes.

Answers: 1. Fat (butter or margarine); 2. Sugar (brown); 3. Spice (1/2 teaspoon cinnamon and 1/4 teaspoon nutmeg); 4. Egg; 5. Flour; 6. Curds and Whey (sour milk); 7. A bowl; 8. Spoon

from the kitchen of Lynette Wright

Peanut Butter Cocoa Cookies

2 pounds 10x sugar
1 cup cocoa

Melt in double boiler:
1 pound unsalted butter
1 pound cheese
1 pound chunky peanut butter.

Mix by hand. Place on cookie sheet and pat flat. Cool in refrigerator approximately 10 minutes. Take out cut and serve. If oil appears on top, pat with paper towel.

from the kitchen of Vagnita Morris,
Newport News, Virginia

Holly Leaves

40 large marshmallows
1 stick margarine
1 teaspoon vanilla

Melt these ingredients in microwave or double boiler. Add one small bottle green food coloring (1 ounce). Pour 5 cups cornflakes into large bowl. Pour marshmallow mixture over it and work in to cover. Drop in small bunches on waxed paper. Add cinnamon dots to resemble berries. Allow to dry. These are decorative around a punch bowl or cookie tray. They are delicious too, but might give you green teeth.

from the kitchen of Barbara Farris

Coconut Igloos

1 stick butter
1 cup sugar
1-1pound 4 ounce can crushed pineapple, drained
1 cup dark raisins, chopped
1 cup pecans, chopped
1-8 ounce box butter cookies
1 pint whipping cream
grated coconut

Cream butter and sugar. Add pineapple, raisins and nuts. Spread mixture between cookies, using 3 to a group. Let stand at room temperature. Whip cream and sweeten to taste. Add a few drops of vanilla, if desired.

Frost top and sides of each igloo with cream and sprinkle with coconut. (Top with maraschino cherry, if desired). Let stand in refrigerator for several hours before serving. Serves 16.

Peach Leather

(An Old-Fashioned Peach Candy)

Puree fully ripe peaches in blender until very smooth. Add 2 teaspoons asorbic acid powder and 2 tablespoons of sugar per quart of puree, if desired. Heat just to boiling to dissolve sugar and to prevent darkening.

Lightly oil or spray with non-stick coating a jelly roll pan or cookie sheet with low sides. Spread puree thinly on pans (about 1/4" deep).
Bake in 180 degree oven for 4-6 hours or until no longer tacky to the touch. Run knife around edges and peel out of the pan. Roll up or out, if desired.

May be stored in an airtight container for several weeks at room temperature, several months in the refrigerator or several years in the freezer.

Five Pound Candy

3 pounds granulated sugar
1/2 pound butter
1 large can milk
1 small can milk
1 1/2 pounds can white Karo syrup or bottle
1 pound English walnuts

Mix all ingredients, except nuts; cook until the mixture will form a soft ball when dropped in water; beat constantly until stiff enough to pour on buttered plate, add walnut meats, let cool and cut in squares.
This recipe will make 5 pounds candy, especially good at Christmas time.

Church Windows

12 ounce semi-sweet chocolate chips
10 ounce colored miniature marshmallows
7 ounce package coconut
1/4 pound (stick) margarine
1 cup walnuts, chopped

Melt chocolate chips and margarine in top of double boiler over hot water. Cool; add nuts and marshmallows. Shape into 2 or 3 logs on waxed paper. Roll in coconut and chill 24 hours. Slice and serve. Note: can also be rolled in chopped nuts.

from the kitchen of Barbara Forrister
Darien, Georgia

Brown Sugar Cookies

1 pound brown sugar
3 eggs
1 cup shortening
6 tablespoons boiling water
1 teaspoon soda in the water
3 1/2 cups flour
1 teaspoon salt
vanilla to taste

Mix well, roll thin and cut with cookie cutter. Bake in hot oven, 10 to 12 minutes.

Butter Cookies

1 cup butter
1/4 cup brown sugar
1/2 cup sugar
1 egg yolk
2 cups flour

Cream butter and gradually add sugars. Add egg yolk, and then flour, mixing well after each addition. Roll dough into walnut size balls. Place on ungreased cookie sheet and press down with a fork one time (not crisscross as you would with peanut butter cookies). Bake at 325 degrees until light brown, about 10 minutes.

Greek Christmas Cookies

1 cup butter
2 cups powdered sugar
1 egg yolk
2 cups sifted flour
1 teaspoon cinnamon
1 teaspoon cloves
1/8 teaspoon salt
1/2 teaspoon nutmeg
2 cups almonds, finely ground and unblanced
candied cherries, halved

Cream butter and sugar until light and fluffy. Add egg yolk and all other ingredients, except cherries. Knead well with hands or spoon. (This dough is stiff.) Shape in small balls with hands dusted with powdered sugar. Put on baking sheets 2 inches apart. Press half a cherry in center of each cookie.
Bake at 350 degrees until golden brown, about 15 minutes. Cool on racks. Makes 40.

Desserts

A Sister Is

A perfect playmate, friend for life, and cohort in childhood crimes.
Laughter and pranks throughout the day; a kiss on the cheek at bedtime.

A confidante, a pillar of strength, until your burdens are lifted;
Seeming to be able to read your mind, at this she's truly gifted.

Bossy in her own way, she says she knows what's best for you.
In the end, when all is said and done, grudgingly you know it's true.

The Lord created a jewel with sparkle and colors so intense,
He gave her the heart of an angel, and so much common sense.

She's all the seasons rolled into one
A magnificent woman, look what God's done!

Sharon Strickland

Elizabeth

There are many women with this name that quickly come to mind,
Just look back in the history books or on the big screen, this name you will find.

I want to tell you a story of the Elizabeth I know,
Of how she turned fertile fields in four young minds, then planted dreams and watched them grow.

A tiny woman of Dutch decent with a little English thrown in on the side,
Short in stature, a happy nature and grey eyes that opened wide.

Widowed young, single mom, before this was popular,
Then after that, four grandchildren that depended solely on her.

She never traveled outside her realm, she didn't seem to have the need,
And even though her means were limited no one was turned away, she was "a friend indeed."

She taught us about prejudice, being poor we learned this first hand,
Never judge a person by wealth or color, but how morally correct they stand.

She was poor in many ways, but wealthy in many others,
She gave hope to many, taught us how to love and respect one another.

She surely changed the lives of four youngsters, she was all we had you see.
Without this grand lady, where would we four be?

No, she's never been on the silver screen, but she's an Oscar winner in our eyes,
Her crown was loyalty, love, humility and selfless sacrifice.

In loving memory of dear sissy, she is truly missed.

Sharon Strickland

Scripture Cake

1)	1 cup Judges 5:25	(butter)
2)	2 cups Jeremiah 6:20	(sugar)
3)	6 Jeremiah 17:11	(eggs)
4)	2 tablespoons Samuel 14:25	(honey)
5)	4 1/2 cups I Kings 4:22	(flour)
6)	2 teaspoons Amos 4:5	(baking powder)
7)	1 pinch Leviticus 2:15	(salt)
8)	1 cup Judges 4:19	(milk)
9)	2 cups I Samuel 30:12	(raisins)
10)	2 cups Nahum 3:12, chopped	(figs)
11)	2 cups Numbers 17:8, slivered	(almonds)

Make it a family project to look up the ingredients. All are found in the Bible (King James Version).

Cream first two ingredients. Add third, one at a time. Add fourth ingredient and beat well. Mix ingredients 5, 6 & 7 and add alternately with ingredient number 8. Stir in ingredients 9, 10 & 11. Bake in two greased loaf pans at 350 degrees for about one hour or until done.

from the kitchen of Lynette Wright

Peanut Butter Pound Cake

2 sticks margarine, softened
2 cups white sugar
1 cup brown sugar
1/2 cup peanut butter
5 eggs
3 cups plain flour
1/2 teaspoon baking powder
1/2 teaspoon salt
1/4 teaspoon soda
1 cup milk
1/2 teaspoon vanilla

Blend margarine, sugars and peanut butter. Add eggs, one at a time, blending well after each addition. Add flour, baking powder, salt and soda. Combine milk and vanilla. Add flour and milk alternating each one; mix well. Bake at 325 degrees for 1 1/2 hours.

Jam Cake

(70 Year Old Recipe)

3 cups flour
6 eggs
2 cups sugar
1/2 cup butter
1 teaspoon soda
1 cup buttermilk
2 packages dates
1 box raisins
2 packages figs
2 cups blackberry jam
1 teaspoon spice
1 teaspoon cinnamon

Mix flour, eggs, sugar, butter, soda and buttermilk to make batter. Cut up fruit and add to batter; mix well. Bake same way as fruit cake.

Filling (or topping):
2 cups sugar
1 cup milk
1/2 cup butter
1 egg white, beaten

Cook until mixture drops from spoon in a thick string. Whip together with 1 beaten egg white.

Burnt Leather Cake

2 1/2 cups sifted flour
2 teaspoons baking powder
1/2 teaspoon salt
1/2 cup butter or other shortening
1 1/2 cups white sugar
3 egg yolks, well-beaten
1 cup water
2 teaspoons vanilla
3 tablespoons burnt sugar syrup
3 egg whites, stiffly beaten

To make burnt sugar syrup: place 1 cup brown sugar in skillet over medium flame and stir constantly until melted and almost black. Add 1 cup boiling water and cook until it is like molasses.

Sift flour once and measure: add baking powder and salt; sift again 3 times. Cream shortening thoroughly; add sugar gradually and cream together until light and fluffy. Add egg yolks and heat well; add flour alternately with water, small amount at a time. Beat after each addition until smooth. Add vanilla. Add 3 tablespoons burnt sugar syrup, blend. Fold in egg whites.

Bake in large sheet pan in moderate oven, 375 degrees, for 25 minutes or longer. Spread with icing.

Icing Recipe:

2 cups white sugar
2 egg whites, beaten
3 tablespoons burnt sugar syrup

Cook sugar until it threads in cold water. Pour over beaten egg whites. Add burnt sugar syrup.

Banana Nut Pound Cake

Mix together:
1 1/2 cups oil
2 1/2 cups sugar
Sift together:
3 cups flour
1 teaspoon soda
3/4 teaspoon salt

Add 3 eggs, well-beaten. Blend in blender or mix together:

1/2 cup buttermilk
1 1/2 cups mashed bananas (about 3)
1 teaspoon vanilla

Add to sugar and oil mixture; then add all to flour mixture. Fold in 1 cup coconut and 1 cup chopped pecans. Bake at 325 degrees for 1 hour and 20 minutes.

Sour Cream Pound Cake

2 sticks butter or margarine
3 cups sugar
6 eggs
3 cups plain flour
1/4 teaspoon soda
1/2 pint sour cream
1 teaspoon vanilla
1 teaspoon lemon flavoring

Cream butter or margarine and sugar. Add eggs, one at a time, beating well after each addition. Add flavorings, flour, soda and salt which has been sifted together, alternating with milk. Pour in tube pan which has been greased and floured. Bake for 1 hour and 10 minutes in 325 degree oven.

Old Fashioned Pound Cake

1 cup butter
2 cups sugar
3 cups flour
1 cup milk
5 eggs
1 teaspoon vanilla
2 teaspoons baking powder

Cream butter and sugar. Add eggs one at a time beating well after each addition. Add flour and baking powder alternately with milk. Add vanilla. Bake in 350 degree oven about 1 hour and 15 minutes.

Chocolate Pound Cake

2 sticks butter
1/2 cup Crisco
3 cups sugar
5 eggs
1 cup milk
2 teaspoons vanilla
1/2 teaspoon salt
3 cups flour
1/2 teaspoon baking powder
4 to 5 heaping tablespoons cocoa

Cream butter and Crisco with sugar. Add eggs, one at a time, beating thoroughly after each. Combine flour, salt, baking powder and cocoa. Add alternately with milk, beginning and ending with dry ingredients. Blend in vanilla. Bake in greased and floured tube pan for 1 1/2 to2 hours in 275 degree oven.

Hickory Nut Cake

5 egg whites
1 cup butter
1 cup milk
3 1/2 cups Swans Down cake flour
3 teaspoons baking powder
2 cups sugar
2 teaspoons vanilla
2 cups Hickory nut meats, rolled in flour

Mix as any white cake, adding beaten egg whites and nuts last. Bake in greased and floured, tube pan in moderate oven until done. Ice with white or mocha frosting made with confectioners' sugar.

Pineapple Delight Cake

1-16 ounce sour cream
1 1/2 cup sugar
2-15 1/2 ounce cans crushed pineapple, drained

Combine ingredients and refrigerate overnight, for cake filling and topping.

1 stick butter
1 stick margarine
2 cups sugar
eggs
3 cups all-purpose flour
3 teaspoons baking powder
1 teaspoon salt
1 cup milk
1 teaspoon pineapple 4 or vanilla flavoring
1-8 ounce Cool Whip

Cream butter, margarine and sugar. Add eggs, one at a time. Sift flour, baking powder and salt. Add dry ingredients alternately with milk. Add flavoring and beat about 1 minute. Divide batter into 2 (9-inch) layer pans. Bake at 350 degrees for 30 to 35 minutes. Cool 10 minutes. Remove from pans. Cool and split layers to make 4 layers. Reserve 1 1/2 cups of filling. Spread remainder between layers.
To reserved filling, fold in thawed Cool Whip. Spread over cake top and sides. Store covered! Refrigerate overnight until served.

Southern White Fruit Cake

1 2/3 cup white raisins
1 cup candied citron
1 cup cherries
1 cup pineapple peel
1 cup lemon peel
2/3 cup shortening
  part butter for flavor)
1 1/3 cup sugar
2 2/3 cups Gold
  Medal flour
1 1/3 teaspoon salt
2 cups almonds,
  blanced
2/3 cup water
6 egg whites

First: Wash raisins, then "puff" them by dropping them into water at the boiling point, turning off heat, and letting them stand about 15 minutes. Drain and dry.

Now: Prepare the other fruit. Shave the citron thinly with a sharp knife; cut the cherries in halves, then in fourths. Cut the pineapple in thin wedges, about the size of halves of cherries; using scissors, cut the oranges and lemon peels into thin strips. Cut the almonds into small pieces and "toast" them by placing in pan in the oven (light brown).

Now: Cream the shortening, add sugar gradually and cream until fluffy. Sift flour, baking powder, and salt together; mix about 1 cup of this mixture with the mixed fruit and nuts; add the remainder of flour mixture to the creamed mixture, alternately with water.

Now: Stir in the fruit and nuts. Fold in egg whites which have been beaten until stiff, but not dry.

Now: Line pan with 2 thicknesses of heavy plain paper and grease well. Pour in the batter; bake 1 3/4 to 2 hours. Oven 300 degrees. A paper may be placed over the top of pan in the last half hour. Wrap in a cloth soaked in light wine, put in covered jar. Keep in cool place.

Gingerbread

2 cups dark molasses
1 cup brown sugar
1 cup butter
4 eggs
2 tablespoons ground ginger
2 teaspoons ground cinnamon
1 cup buttermilk
2 teaspoons (scant) soda
1 teaspoon baking powder
4 cups flour

Cream together butter and sugar; add eggs; beat well. Sift together flour, spices and baking powder. Put soda in buttermilk; add dry ingredients alternately with liquid to creamed mixture; add molasses. Bake in greased loaf pan at 350 degrees until done.

Brownies and Icing

1 stick margarine
1/2 cup shortening
2 cups sugar
4 whole eggs
1 cup flour
1/2 cup cocoa
1 teaspoon vanilla
1/2 cup evaporated milk
1 cup black walnuts (optional)

Cream margarine and shortening; add sugar and cream thoroughly. Add eggs, one at a time, then vanilla. Add dry ingredients alternately with milk. Add nuts. Pour into a greased and floured 9 x 13-inch pan. Bake at 350 degrees for 25 to 30 minutes. Don't overbake!

Icing

1 box powdered sugar
1 stick margarine
1 teaspoon vanilla
2 tablespoons cocoa
milk to spread

Mix and spread over brownies while hot, just from the oven. Let cool in pan. Cut in desired size and store in tins. Makes 4 dozen 1 1/2-inch squares.

Chocolate Fudge Cake

1/2 cup butter
  (1/4 pound)
3 eggs, separated
2 1/2 cups white sugar
5 1/2 large squares chocolate
 (5 1/2 ounce)
2 1/2 cups Swans Down
  cake flour
1 1/2 cups sweet milk
2 teaspoons baking
  powder
1 cup nut meats
  (or more)
2 teaspoons vanilla
1/4 teaspoon salt

Cream butter, add egg yolks; add sugar and beat well. Add flour and milk; add melted chocolate, nut meats, vanilla and salt. Fold in beaten egg whites. Add baking powder last. Bake in 9-inch pans 375 degrees, time it takes for large devil's food.

Cocoa Frosting

12 tablespoons brown sugar
6 tablespoons cocoa
6 tablespoons butter
6 tablespoons cream

Put all in pan, melt, then add powdered sugar to spread.

Texas Pecan Cake

1 pound butter
  (unsalted)
2 1/2 cups sugar
6 eggs, well-beaten
1 tablespoon lemon extract
4 cups sifted all-purpose flour
1 1/2 teaspoons
  baking powder
4 cups fresh pecan
  halves
2 cups white raisins

Heat oven to 300 degrees. Grease and flour 10-inch tube pan. Blend butter and sugar in a large bowl until light and fluffy. Gradually add eggs and lemon extract and beat until blended. Sift flour and baking powder three times. Add nuts and raisins to flour. Gradually add flour mixture to creamed mixture and blend thoroughly. Pour into prepared pan. Bake 1 1/2 to 2 hours. Cool 15 minutes; remove from pan and cool completely.

Pound Cake

3 sticks margarine
3 cups sugar
3 cups flour
5 eggs
1 cup milk
1 teaspoon lemon flavoring
2 teaspoons vanilla flavoring

Mix ingredients together well. Cook 1 hour and 15 minutes at 325 or 350 degrees according to your oven.

Winter Brunch Fruit Compote

1 large can peach slices
1 large can pineapple chunks
1 large can sliced pears
1/2 bottle maraschino cherries
1/3 cup butter
3/4 cup light brown sugar
2 teaspoons chili powder

Melt butter and sugar. Add chili powder and spoon over drained fruit. Bake uncovered in a 325 degree oven for 60 minutes. Refrigerate overnight. Reheat in a 350 degree oven for 30 minutes. Serves 12.

a moon pie and a coke is
one step closer to heaven.

Whiskey Cake

1 package Duncan Hines Golden Butter cake mix
3/4 cup sugar
3/4 cup vegetable oil
4 eggs
1 cup buttermilk
4 tablespoons Bourbon whiskey
2 tablespoons vanilla extract (pure)
2 tablespoons dark brown sugar
2 tablespoons ground cinnamon

Combine cake mix with sugar, eggs, oil, buttermilk; add Bourbon and vanilla; mix well.

Grease bundt pan with Crisco. Pour 1/2 of batter into bundt pan and sprinkle brown sugar and cinnamon over batter. Pour the rest of the batter into bundt pan. Bake about 1 hour at 350 degrees. Test for doneness. Cool in pan for about 30 minutes.

Cherry Crown

2 cups canned water-packed cherries
2 envelopes low-calorie lemon-flavored gelatin

Drain cherries and measure juice. Add enough boiling water to make 2 cups of liquid. Add gelatin and stir until dissolved.

Chill for about 30 minutes or until slightly thickened. Stir in cherries. Pour into 6 individual molds and chill for 1 hour or until firm.

Pumpkin Cake Roll

Beat 3 eggs at high speed for 5 minutes. Gradually add 1 cup sugar. Stir in 2/3 cup pumpkin and 1 teaspoon lemon juice. Sift together 3/4 cup flour, 1 teaspoon baking powder, 2 teaspoons cinnamon, 1 teaspoon ginger, 1/2 teaspoon nutmeg, 1/2 teaspoon salt. Fold above ingredients into pumpkin mixture. Spread into wax paper lined 15 x 10 x1-inch cookie sheet.

Top with 1 cup finely chopped nuts. Bake 15 minutes at 375 degrees. Turn on a towel sprinkled with powdered sugar. Roll cake and towel together. Cool completely. Unroll and spread with 1 cup powdered sugar, 6 ounces cream cheese, 4 tablespoons butter or oleo and 1/2 teaspoon vanilla. Beat until smooth and spread on cake.

Then roll cake together again and chill.

from the kitchen of Susan Kapitan Richards,
mother of Donna Durgin

Fruit Cocktail Cake

2 cups flour
1 1/2 cups sugar
2 teaspoons soda
1/2 teaspoon salt
16-17 ounces fruit cocktail, juice included
2 eggs
1 teaspoon vanilla

Blend above ingredients and pour into ungreased 9 x 13-inch pan. Bake 375 degrees for 40 minutes.

Sauce

3/4 cup sugar
1/2 cup chopped nuts
1 teaspoon vanilla
1/2 cup coconut
1/2 cup butter or margarine
1/2 cup canned cream

Combine in a saucepan, bring to a boil and boil for 2 minutes. Pour over cake while both are still warm.

Pumpkin Cheesecake

3-8 ounce packages cream cheese
1/4 cup light brown sugar
1 teaspoon cornstarch
1/4 teaspoon cinnamon
1/2 teaspoon nutmeg
2/3 cup undiluted evaporated milk
1 cup sugar
1 3/4 cup pumpkin
2 eggs
1 graham cracker pie crust

Beat cream cheese, sugar and brown sugar in a bowl until fluffy. Beat in pumpkin, eggs and evaporated milk. Add cornstarch, cinnamon and nutmeg (beat well). Pour into crust. Bake in preheated oven at 350 degrees for 1 hour or until edge is set.

Topping

2 cups sour cream (room temperature)
1/4 to 1/3 cup sugar
1 teaspoon vanilla

Combine sour cream, vanilla and sugar in small bowl. Spread onto warm cheesecake. Return to 350 degree oven and bake for 5 minutes. Cool on wire rack. Chill several hours.

Bread Pudding

4 cups of bread crumbs
1 1/2 cups sugar
1 teaspoon cinnamon
2 eggs
4 tablespoons melted margarine
1 #2 can crushed pineapple with juice
1 cup raisins
1/2 cup milk (half/half is best)

Combine all ingredients and pour into well greased baking pan. Bake in a preheated oven at 375 degrees for 1 hour or until straw inserted comes out clean.

from the kitchen of Nana Whitaker

Fresh Apple Cake

Mix 1 cup oil (room temperature), 2 cups well-packed brown sugar, 4 large eggs and 1 teaspoon vanilla. Mix well at low speed until creamy smooth.

Stir together 1 1/4 cups oat flour, 1 1/4 cups brown rice flour, 1 teaspoon salt, and 1 tablespoon baking powder. Add half of the dry ingredients to the creamed mixture, beating well. Then add the rest of the dry ingredients, finishing mixing by hand. Fold through 1 cup black walnuts and 3 cups coarsely chopped, peeled raw apples.

Bake in greased, wax paper lined 9 x 13-inch glass baking dish at 350 degrees for about 55 minutes. If the cake starts to get too brown, turn the temperature down for the last few minutes.

Chill. Serve with whipped cream or cover with Jelled Whipped Cream.

Jelled Whipped Cream

Soak 1 teaspoon unflavored gelatin in 2 tablespoons cold water. Melt over hot water. Pour into 1 cup whipping cream, stirring vigorously. Chill until firm. Beat until you have whipped cream. Spread on cake, fill cream puffs, then refrigerate to set gelatin.

Variations: flavor with chocolate syrup, carob drink mix or your favorite flavoring with honey or brown sugar. Maple syrup is good.

Littlest Angel Cake

Mix 1 cup sifted WW flour with 3/4 cup well-packed brown sugar using the back of the spoon to crush and mix sugar lumps. Put mixture into sifter. (Do not use a double sifter.)

Beat together 1 1/2 cups egg whites, 1 1/2 teaspoons cream of tartar, 1/4 teaspoon salt, 1 teaspoon vanilla and 1/2 teaspoon almond flavoring until stiff but still glossy. Add 3/4 cup well-packed brown sugar in 3 parts, beating well each time. Use a large spoon in a folding action to make sure everything is mixed well. Fold in flour with the large spoon, sifting a little over the top and gently folding in.

Pour into ungreased angel food cake pan, smoothing the top. Bake at 375 degrees for about 35 minutes. Touch the top gently to see if cake is done.

Invert pan and cool completely. Then remove from pan.

Variations: ice with Jelled Whipped Cream (see previous page for recipe), plain or chocolate or serve with fruit and whipped cream.
You may fill the cake with Jelled Whipped Cream. Slice a thin layer off the top, then hollow out the center. Fill and cover again with the top slice. Chill and serve.
Omit almond flavoring and increase vanilla to 1 1/2 teaspoons.
Substitute 1/4 cup cocoa (or carob powder) for an equal amount of flour, and omit almond flavoring.
Substitute 1/2 cup each sifted brown rice flour and oat flour in place of WW flour.

from the kitchen of Lynette Wright

Glazed Wheat Carrot Torte

2 tablespoons softened butter or margarine
2 1/4 cups regular wheat germ, divided
2/3 cup firmly packed, grated carrots (2 large)
1/2 cup almonds, blanced and ground
1/4 cup unsifted all-purpose flour
6 eggs, separated
1 1/4 cups sugar
1/4 cup orange juice
1 tablespoon grated orange rind
1/2 teaspoon salt
1/2 teaspoon cinnamon

Grease a 9-inch springform pan with butter. Sprinkle pan evenly with 1/4 cup wheat germ. Combine 2 cups wheat germ, carrots, almonds and flour on waxed paper. Stir well to blend. Beat egg whites in small bowl until stiff peaks form. Combine egg yolks, sugar, orange juice, orange rind, salt and cinnamon in large bowl. Beat well. Add blended dry ingredients to egg yolk mixture. Stir well to blend. Fold in beaten egg whites. Pour batter into prepared pan.
Bake at 350 degrees for 55 to 60 minutes, until cake tester inserted in center comes out clean. Remove from pan. Cool on rack. Spread Orange Glaze on torte, letting glaze drizzle down sides. Makes 16 to 20 servings.

Orange Glaze

3/4 cup sugar
4 tablespoons cornstarch
2 teaspoon grated orange rind
1 teaspoon grated lemon rind
1 cup orange juice

Combine sugar, cornstarch, orange rind and lemon rind in small saucepan. Stir well to blend. Add orange juice slowly, stirring well . Cook over low heat, stirring constantly until thickened and glossy. Remove from heat. Stir in 2 tablespoons butter or margarine. Cool slightly, about 5 minutes.

from the kitchen of Lynette Wright

Blueberry Crumb Cake

1 1/2 cups sugar
2 eggs
1/2 cup oil
4 cups flour
4 teaspoons baking powder
1 cup milk
2 cans drained blueberries

Mix sugar and oil; add eggs. Add milk and dry ingredients. Fold in drained blueberries. Put batter in greased and floured 9 x 13-inch pan. Sprinkle on topping. Bake at 350 degrees for 40 to 50 minutes.

Topping

2/3 cup flour
1/2 cup sugar
2 teaspoons cinnamon
1/2 cup margarine

Fresh Apple Cake

Mix 1 1/2 cups oil (room temperature), 2 cups well-packed brown sugar, 2 large eggs and 1 teaspoon vanilla. Beat well until creamy smooth.

Stir together 2 1/2 cups sifted WW flour, 1 teaspoon salt and 1 tablespoon baking powder. Add dry ingredients to creamed mixture in small amounts, beating well each time. Finish by hand, as this mixture will be very thick. Fold in 1 cup black walnuts and 3 cups chopped raw apples.

Bake in greased 9 x 13-inch glass baking dish at 350 degrees for 55 to 60 minutes. Chill. Serve with whipped cream or ice with Jelled Whipped Cream (see recipe on page144).

Pecan Pie

2-8 inch pie shells
1/4 cup butter
2 tablespoons white vinegar
1 1/2 cups chopped pecans
2 cups sugar
2 tablespoons plain flour
4 eggs, well-beaten
2 tablespoons cold water

Cream sugar and butter, then add flour, vinegar and water. Mix well, add eggs and nuts. Bake at 350 degrees until done (about 1 hour).

Pie Crust

1 1/4 cups plain flour
1 stick butter
2 tablespoons vinegar

Mix all ingredients together until dough forms. Makes enough for one crust.

Cool and Easy Lemon Chiffon Pie

1/4 teaspoon cream of tartar
3 egg whites
few drops of yellow food coloring
1-14 ounce can Eagle Brand Sweetened Condensed Milk (not evaporated)
1/3 cup lemon juice
1 graham cracker ready made crust

In medium bowl, combine sweetened condensed milk, lemon juice and food coloring. Mix well. In small bowl, beat egg whites with cream of tartar until stiff, but not dry. Gently fold into sweetened condensed milk mixture. Pour into crust. Chill 3 hours or until set. Refrigerate leftovers.

Buttermilk Pie

(in use since 1910)

3 eggs (reserving whites of two for meringue)
2 cups buttermilk
1/4 cup flour
1 cup sugar
1 teaspoon vanilla

Beat the two egg yolks and whole egg until frothy; add sugar gradually until all is used; add the flour to the mixture until well blended. Add vanilla extract. Cook on top of stove until thick enough to spread nicely in a previously baked pie crust. Beat whites until very stiff; add 2 tablespoons sugar and beat in the whites and spread on pie. Brown meringue in oven.

Cheese or Transparent Pie

6 yolks of eggs
1 cup sugar
1/2 cup boiling water
1/2 cup butter
1/2 teaspoon vanilla

Beat yolks of eggs until foamy, adding sugar gradually. Add the butter and mix. Stir in boiling water and vanilla. Bake in a moderate oven until custard is firm and crust brown.

Pinto Bean Pie

1 cup cooked pinto beans, mashed with liquid
1 cup Angel Flake coconut
1 cup chopped nuts
4 eggs
1 tablespoon vanilla
2 cups sugar
2 sticks margarine, melted
2 unbaked pie shells

Mix well. Bake 1 hour at 300 degrees.

Rhubarb Pie

4 cups rhubarb, cut up
6 tablespoons flour
2-2 1/2 cups sugar
1 egg
1 tablespoon butter

Mix all and heap in 9-inch pie dough lined pie pan. Dot with butter. Bake 450 degrees for 15 minutes or 350 degree for 45 minutes. Can use top crust or crumb topping.

from the kitchen of Joan Meager

Carolina Coffee Cake

1/2 cup walnuts
1/2 cup pecans
1/2 cup almonds
2 cups loose brown sugar
2 1/2 cups flour
2 teaspoons baking powder
1 teaspoon salt
3 teaspoons cinnamon
2 sticks butter
1/2 cup sugar
2 packages vanilla pudding (1-4.6 ounce/1-3 ounce size)
1 teaspoon vanilla
4 eggs
1 cup water

In mixer, beat or cream softened butter until fluffy. Add 1/2 cup sugar and pudding mix (dry from package). Beat until smooth. Add vanilla and eggs. In separate bowl, add brown sugar and 1/2 of the cinnamon. Ground all nuts finely and add to brown sugar. Set aside. In another bowl, mix together flour, baking powder and rest of cinnamon. Alternately mix flour mixture into egg mixture with water. Blend thoroughly. Pour half of mix into 2 8 x 8-inch baking pans (greased). Top with nut mixture. Cover with remaining batter. Bake at 350 degrees for 40-45 minutes.

from the kitchen of Judith Frampton,
Prospect Hill Inn

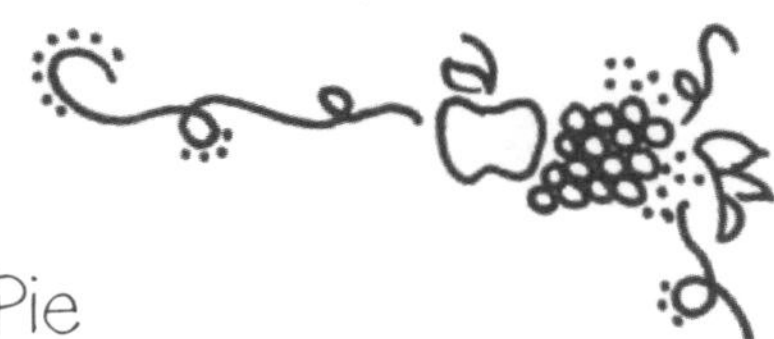

Zucchini Pie

(tastes like apple)

2 rounded teaspoons flour
1/8 teaspoon salt
1/8 teaspoon nutmeg
1 1/4 cups sugar
1 1/2 teaspoons cinnamon
1 1/2 teaspoons cream of tartar
2 1/2 tablespoons lemon juice
4-5 cups sliced zucchini

Combine first seven ingredients. Peel zucchini, cut lengthwise and remove pulp and seeds. Slice thin as for apple pie. Cook in own juice until transparent but not mushy. Drain thoroughly and cool. Combine all, place in 10-inch pie shell. Dot with butter. Use top crust or crumb topping. Bake at 400 degrees for 40-45 minutes.

Banana Pudding

1 box instant vanilla pudding
1 box vanilla wafers (7.25 ounce)
4 bananas, sliced
2 eggs
1 cup sugar
1 teaspoon vanilla flavoring
1-8 ounce cool whip

Mix pudding according to directions on box. Add eggs, sugar, vanilla flavoring and one-half of the cool whip. Arrange wafers, sliced bananas and pudding in layers in 2 quart casserole ending with a layer of pudding on top. Add remaining cool whip and a few vanilla wafers. Serves 8.

from the kitchen of Glenda Claxton

Pie Dough

6 cups flour
2 1/2 cups butter-flavored Crisco
2 teaspoons salt

Put one egg and 1 tablespoon vinegar in a 1 cup measuring cup. Stir, then fill with cold water.

Mix flour and salt; add room temperature shortening and blend with pastry blender. Make a hole and pour in liquid. Mix with a fork. Will be moist. Chill before rolling. Roll out like pie dough.

Very flaky - if tears mends easily, kinda sticky

Make 4 double crusts. Recipe is at least 70 years old.

from the kitchen of Joan Meager

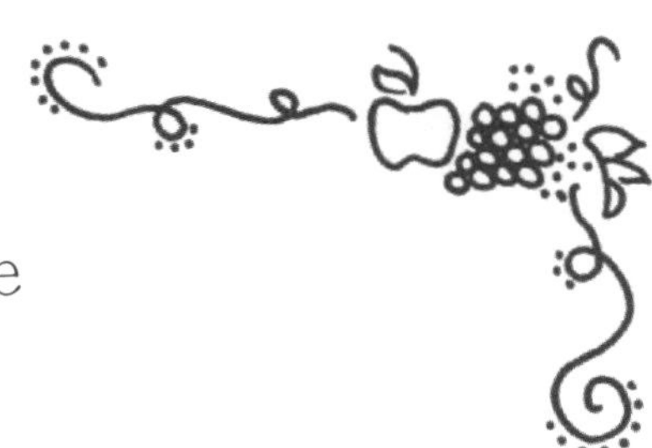

Jello Pie

graham crackers
small jello-nutrasweet
15 ounce can applesauce
Cool Whip

Mix jello and applesauce. Bottom of dish put layer of crackers, spread mix, layer crackers, spread mix, layer crackers and top with Cool Whip. Refrigerate.

Lemon Luscious Pie

(this recipe won a baking contest)

9" Pie Pastry

1 1/2 cups flour
1/4-1/2 teaspoon salt
1/2 cup shortening and 2 tablespoons butter
4-5 tablespoons cold water

Filling

1 cup sugar
3 tablespoons cornstarch
1/4 cup fresh lemon juice
lemon rind, grated from one lemon
1/4 cup butter
3 egg yolks

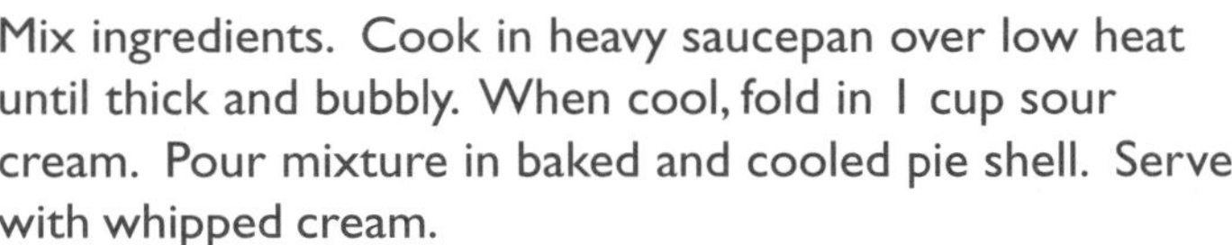

Mix ingredients. Cook in heavy saucepan over low heat until thick and bubbly. When cool, fold in 1 cup sour cream. Pour mixture in baked and cooled pie shell. Serve with whipped cream.

from the kitchen of Donna Durgin

Vermont Honey-Apple Pie

Pastry
2 cups unbleached wheat flour
1/2 teaspoon salt
2/3 cup shortening
3-4 tablespoons butter
5-7 tablespoons cold water

Filling
8-9 tart apples (macintosh)
1/2 cup honey (scant)
1 tablespoon cinnamon
2 1/2 tablespoons flour
juice of half lemon (or whole lemon if lemon is small)
dash nutmeg
2 tablespoons batter to dot top of apples

Prepare pastry. Divide in 1/2. Roll out. Spread half of pastry in 9-inch pie plate. Mix ingredients with peeled and thinly sliced apples. Dot top with butter. Put top crust over apples and seal. Make decorative edges. Bake at 400 degrees for 50 minutes.

from the kitchen of Donna Durgin

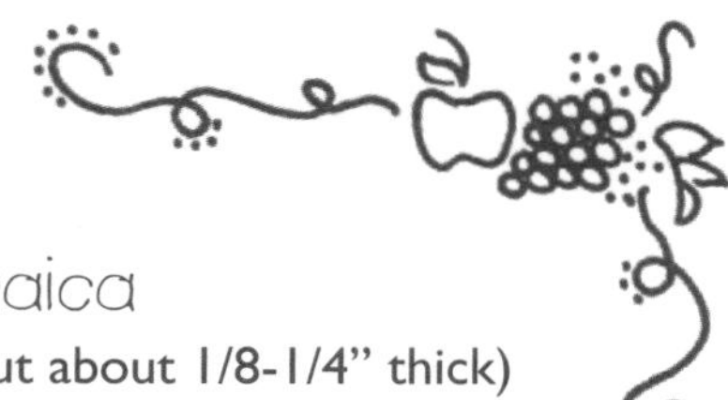

Creme Jamaica

3 large or 4 medium ripe bananas (cut about 1/8-1/4" thick)
1 1/2 ounces Southern Comfort
1 ounce fresh lemon juice
1 1/2 ounces sugar

Toss gently and let sit at room temperature for about 1 hour, tossing occasionally.

Pudding

1 cup milk
1 ounce cornstarch
3 ounces sugar
1 1/2 ounces water

Mix over double boiler. Bring milk to a boil. Add cornstarch sugar water mix while stirring vigorously with whisk and then for 3 more minutes. You should have a smooth - like a thick sauce pudding. You may add 1 ounce of butter, a few drops of pure vanilla extract and an egg yolk (well-beaten) with a little heavy cream. You now have what the pros call a creame "patisiere". Put into a container and seal with thin plastic touching the pudding to prevent a skin. Put into the refrigerator to set at least 5 hours. To assemble, put bananas in a strainer or sift over a bowl to collect the marinade. Whip the pudding to smooth. Make sure there are no lumps. Whip 1/2 pint heavy cream and fold in with smooth pudding. Add marinade while folding to right consistency. You should have some marinade left over. Put bananas in bottom of dish and top with cream.

Peach Ice Cream

- 1 package frozen peaches
- 1 cup milk
- 1/2 cup sugar
- 2 egg yolks, beaten
- 1 cup heavy cream
- 1 teaspoon vanilla extract
- salt

Defrost and drain the peaches. Pour milk into top part of a double boiler; cook over very low heat until a light film forms on top of the milk. Add sugar and salt to the milk; stir until the sugar dissolves. Remove from heat and beat slowly into the egg yolks. Set over hot water; cook, stirring constantly, for 5 minutes or until the mixture coats the spoon. Remove from heat and cool the custard. Then, chill for 30 minutes. Whip the cream until thick, add the peaches, vanilla and chilled custard. Pour into an ice tray and freeze for 1 hour. Turn the ice cream out into a chilled bowl and stir well. Return it to the ice tray and freeze until it is firm enough to serve. Makes about 1 quart.

Peach Custard Ice Cream

- 1 quart whole milk
- 1 cup cream or evaporated milk
- 3 eggs
- 1 cup sugar
- 1 tablespoon vanilla
- 1 tablespoon all-purpose flour
- 1/8 teaspoon salt
- 2 quarts mashed Georgia Peaches

Scald milk and cream. Beat eggs and combine with half of the sugar. Mix flour and salt with remainder of sugar. Blend all with hot milk and cream. Cook until it thickens. Add mashed peaches, 1 tablespoon vanilla and freeze. Makes 1 1/2 gallons.

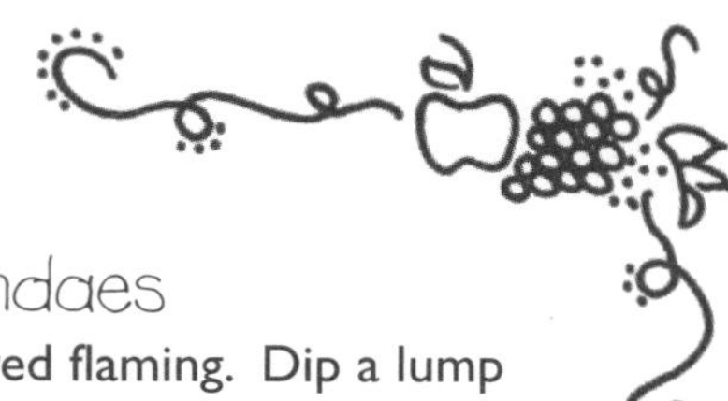

Flaming Sundaes

Any ice cream sundae may be served flaming. Dip a lump of sugar into lemon extract and press it into a marshmallow. Put the marshmallow on the sundae and light the sugar lump. The flaming sugar will toast the marshmallow.

Hot Orange Souffles

1/3 cup plus
 3 tablespoons sugar
6 eggs, separated
2 teaspoons orange rind,
 finely grated
1/4 cup orange juice with
 pulp
1 tablespoon grand
 marnier
confectioner's sugar

Butter the souffle dishes, then sprinkle the side of the dish with sugar (about 1 tablespoon). Set aside. Preheat oven to 450 degrees.

Put egg yolks in medium bowl. Add 1/3 cup sugar, orange rind, juice and grand marnier. Beat briskly with wire whisk. Beat egg white until stiff. Add remaining 2 tablespoons sugar. Fold the egg yolk mixture into whites. Spoon into 1 1/4 cups capacity souffle dishes. Place on cookie sheet and put in oven. Bake 12 minutes; sprinkle with confectioner's sugar.

Orange Sauce

1 cup apricots jam
1/2 cup water
1/2 cup orange sections,
 seeds removed and cut
1 teaspoon orange rind,
 grated
1 tablespoon grand
 marnier

Combine jam and water in saucepan. Cook gently, stirring until blended. Add orange sections and rind. Stir in the grand marnier. Makes 2 cups.

Hot Strawberry Souffles

8 eggs, separated
1 pint strawberries, frozen or fresh
1/2 cup plus 1/3 cup sugar
juice of 1/2 lemon
confectioner's sugar

Preheat oven to 450 degrees. Grease souffle dishes with butter. If you are using frozen strawberries, thaw. If fresh, pick off stems and leaves. Put strawberries into food processor and puree. Put puree into a medium bowl and add egg yolks, 1/2 cup sugar and lemon juice. Beat until well blended. Beat egg whites until stiff and add the remaining sugar while beating. Add 1/2 of egg whites to strawberry mixture and whisk lightly. Add the remaining whites, fold in with spatula.

Put into souffle dishes and put on baking sheet. Reduce oven to 425 degrees and bake 7 minutes. Sprinkle with confectioner's sugar. Serves 4.

Strawberry Sauce

1 pint strawberries, frozen or fresh
juice of 1/2 lemon
1/2 cup sugar
2 tablespoons grand marnier

Rinse and drain strawberries. Put in food processor, add lemon juice and 1/2 cup sugar; blend. Makes 1 1/3 cups.

Chocolate Souffle

3 ounces sweet chocolate
1 ounce unsweetened chocolate
1/2 cup sugar
1 tablespoon coffee liqueur or grand marnier
8 eggs, separated
4 teaspoons confectioner's sugar

Shave chocolate with knife in a mixing bowl. Sit bowl in hot water until chocolate melts. Add half sugar and liqueur; stir to blend. Let cool.

Butter bottom and sides of 1 1/2 cup souffle dishes. Set aside.

Add egg yolk to chocolate mixture and beat until blended. Beat egg whites in another bowl until they form a peak. Gradually add remaining sugar, beating constantly until egg whites peak again. Add 1/2 of the whites to chocolate mixture and fold in quickly with whisk until thoroughly blended. Add remaining whites and fold with rubber spatula. Put into souffle dishes. Bake 10-12 minutes. Sprinkle with confectioner's sugar. Makes 4 servings.

Chocolate Sauce

4 ounces unsweetened chocolate, grated
1 cup water
1/2 cup sugar
1/2 cup heavy cream
1/4 teaspoon ground cinnamon
2 tablespoons coffee liqueur (grand marnier)

Combine chocolate, water and sugar in 2 quart saucepan. Slowly bring to boil, stirring constantly. When chocolate is melted, add cream and cinnamon. Stir to blend. Add liqueur; serve cold or hot. Makes 1 3/4 cups.

Coffee Mousse

1/2 cup butter (room temperature)
2 tablespoons instant espresso coffee powder
2 tablespoons warm water
3/4 cup sugar
5 egg whites
1/4 cup chocolate, finely grated

Put butter in mixing bowl and cream with wire whisk. Blend coffee and water in bowl; add butter and1/4 cup sugar. Beat to blend.

In another mixing bowl, beat egg whites until partially stiff using wire whisk. Gradually add the remaining sugar, beating constantly with whisk. Beat until stiff. Add 1/2 of the whites to the coffee mixture and beat well. Fold in the grated chocolate. Pour in stemmed glasses and chill 4-6 servings.

Strawberries and Pastry Cream

3 egg yolks
1/3 cup sugar
1 tablespoon flour
1 tablespoon cornstarch
2 cups hot milk
1/2 cup vanilla extract
32 red strawberries, 1 pint
sweetened whipped cream

Combine egg yolks, sugar, flour, cornstarch in mixing bowl. Beat well with wire whisk. Add milk, stirring rapidly with whisk; place mixture into saucepan. Stir with wooden spoon over low heat, stirring constantly until the mixture comes to a boil. Do not continue to boil or it could curdle. Stir in vanilla. Pour into 4 small dessert bowls. Let cool.

Trim strawberries. Cut in halves. Put strawberries on top of pastry cream and add a small amount of whipped cream on top of each serving. You can use blueberries instead of strawberries, if desired. Makes 4 servings.

Cheese Souffle

3 tablespoons plus 2 teaspoons butter
1/4 pound swiss cheese
2 cups milk
1/4 cup flour
1/8 teaspoon fresh grated nutmeg
salt and pepper
2 teaspoons cornstarch
1 tablespoon water
6 large eggs, separated
1/4 cup finely grated parmesan cheese

Preheat oven to 375 degrees. Grease a 5 cup souffle dish with 2 teaspoons of butter. Grate cheese. Scald milk without boiling. Melt 3 tablespoons butter in saucepan. Add flour, stir with wire whisk, blending until smooth. Gradually add the hot milk, stirring rapidly with whisk. Add nutmeg; salt and pepper to taste and cook over medium heat about 5 minutes, stirring rapidly. Blend cornstarch and water; add it to the other mixture, stirring briskly. Remove from heat and beat in the egg yolks. Pour mixture into a large mixing bowl. Stir in parmesan cheese. Beat the egg whites until stiff; add half the whites to the sauce and fold them with the whisk. Add remaining whites and grated cheese. Fold with rubber spatula until whites are incorporated. Spoon into souffle pan. Place in oven and bake for 20 minutes. Makes 4 servings. This makes a fancy breakfast when served with different berries.

The best ones we have eaten of these was at Prospect Hill Bed and Breakfast in Waynesville, North Carolina. Our chef was Dennis Frampton, a mighty fine cook and a terrific host, along with wife, Judith. We hope to stay again soon.

Vanilla Cream

1 cup whipping cream
1 tablespoon sugar
1/4 teaspoon pure vanilla extract

Whip the cream until soft peaks form. Add the sugar and vanilla and beat until stiff. Almond extract may be substituted for vanilla. Excellent sweet fruit dip or topping.

No Bake Skedaddles

Mix well in large bowl: 1-3 ounce can chow mein noodles (2 cups) and 1 cup miniature marshmallows. Set aside. Combine in saucepan 3/4 cup sugar, 1/2 cup evaporated milk, 2 tablespoons butter. Bring to a full rolling boil, over high heat, stirring constantly. Remove from heat and add 1-6 ounce package Nestle's semi-sweet chocolate morsels. Stir until melted. Let stand 15 minutes. Pour over noodle mixture and stir until well coated. Drop by heaping teaspoonsful onto waxed paper lined cookie sheet. Chill until set, about 1 hour. Remove from waxed paper. Makes about 3 dozen.

Sharon's Melt in Your Mouth Donuts

3 cups milk
2 packages yeast
4 eggs
1 1/3 cups sugar
1 cup melted shortening
1 1/2 or 2 teaspoons salt
10 cups flour

Dissolve yeast in milk. Mix all together and knead well. Let rise; knead down. Let rise. Roll and cut. Let rise again. Fry in hot fat. Glaze while hot.

Glaze

3/4 cup hot water
1 tablespoon lard
1 tablespoon gelatin
1 1/2 boxes powdered sugar
1 teaspoon vanilla

Soak gelatin in small amount of water. Add lard to hot water; add gelatin then sugar and vanilla. Beat until smooth. Glaze doughnuts.

Sour Cream Apple Pie

Sift together:

2 tablespoons flour
3/4 cup sugar
1/4 teaspoon nutmeg
dash salt

Add: 1 cup sour cream. Beat well and add: 1 egg, unbeaten and 1 teaspoon vanilla. Beat until smooth. Add: 2 cups diced, tart apples. Mix well. Pour into unbaked pie shell. Bake at 400 degrees for 15 minutes. Reduce heat to 350 degrees and bake 30 minutes longer. Remove from oven and top with mixture of:

1/3 cup sugar
1/3 cup flour
1 teaspoon cinnamon
1/4 cup butter or margarine

Return to 400 degree oven; bake 10 more minutes.

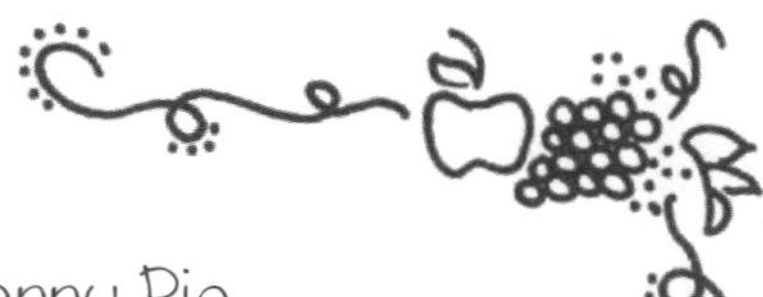

Sissy's Blackberry Pie

1 cup sugar
2 tablespoons (heaping) plain flour
2 eggs, separated
1 tablespoon lemon juice
2 cups berries

Mix together sugar, flour, lemon juice and egg yolks; add berries. Pour into unbaked pie crust, bake until done. When cool use the egg whites for meringue and bake until brown.

Sissy's Blackberry Cake

8 eggs
3 cups flour
1 cup margarine
1 teaspoon soda
3 teaspoons cream of tartar
2 cups sugar
1 1/2 cups blackberry jam
1 cup milk
3 teaspoons cinnamon
2 teaspoons cloves

Mix. Bake in layers about 25 to 30 minutes at 350 degrees. Ice with Caramel Frosting.

Blackberry Pudding

1 1/2 cups cornmeal
1/2 cup flour
1 cup sugar
3 teaspoons baking powder
1 teaspoon salt
1 egg
1 cup milk
1/2 cup butter or margarine, melted
2 cups blackberries, fresh

Preheat oven to 425 degrees. Combine dry ingredients. Add egg, milk and butter. Stir. Add berries, very carefully. Pour into rectangle Pyrex. Bake for 20 to 25 minutes.

Pineapple Sour Cream Pie

3/4 cup sugar
1/2 teaspoon salt
1/4 cup flour
1 tablespoon lemon juice
2 1/2 cups crushed pineapple, undrained
1 cup sour cream
2 slightly beaten egg yolks
1 baked 9" pie shell
2 egg whites for meringue

In saucepan, combine sugar, flour and salt. Stir in next three ingredients. Cook and stir until mixture thickens and comes to boiling. Cook 2 minutes. Stir small amount of hot mixture into egg yolks. Return to heat; stir constantly and cool 2 minutes longer. Spoon into cooled pastry shell. Spread meringue on top of pie, sealing meringue to crust and bake in 350 degree oven until meringue is golden brown.

Fudge Cream Pie

1 baked pie shell
1 1/3 cups sugar
1/4 cup flour
1/4 cup cocoa
1 teaspoon vanilla
1 tall can evaporated milk
3 egg yolks, slightly beaten
1/2 cup pecans, chopped
2 tablespoons butter
1/8 teaspoon salt

Mix sugar, flour, cocoa and salt in saucepan. Stir in evaporated milk. Cook over medium heat until thick, stirring at intervals. Stir small amount of mixture into beaten egg yolks. Return egg-chocolate mixture to heat. Cook and stir until thick. Remove from heat, add pecans, butter or margarine and vanilla. Pour in pie shell and spread meringue over filling. Bake until golden brown.

Meringue

3 egg whites
1/4 teaspoon cream of tartar
1/2 teaspoon vanilla
1/3 cup sugar

Add vanilla and cream of tartar to egg whites. Beat until stiff, gradually add sugar. Continue beating until stiff and glossy.

Apple Dumplings

2 cups flour
2 teaspoons baking powder
1 teaspoon salt
2 tablespoons butter
1 tablespoon lard
7/8 cup milk
1 teaspoon cinnamon
2 tablespoons brown sugar
3 cups tart apples, chopped

Sift dry ingredients (flour, baking powder, salt); knead in lard and butter. Mix with milk; roll out in a sheet 1/2-inch thick, brush with butter and sprinkle with brown sugar and cinnamon. Cover with chopped apples. Roll as you would a jelly roll, cut in 12 equal slices, place slices flat in a buttered pan, cover with the following sauce.

Sauce

1 cup sugar
1 tablespoon butter
1 tablespoon flour
1/2 teaspoon salt
1 cup hot water
1/2 lemon, sliced

Pineapple Delight

3/4 cup white sugar
4 teaspoons melted butter
1 teaspoon vanilla
1 large can crushed pineapple
2 whole eggs, beaten
1/2 pound graham crackers, rolled to dust
1 pint whipping cream
1 cup broken nut meats

Whip cream stiff and add all the ingredients except cracker crumbs. Put half of the cream mixture in a dish or pan; place cracker crumbs, mixed with the melted butter, on top of this. Then place the other half of the cream mixture on top of the cracker crumbs. Place in a cool place until firm or set.

Lemon Meringue Pie

1 1/4 cups sugar
5 tablespoons flour
1/8 teaspoon salt
1 1/2 cups boiling water
1/4 cup lemon juice
(1 lemon)
1 grated lemon rind
1 tablespoon butter
3 egg yolks

Blend sugar, flour and salt; add boiling water and stir until smooth. Cook in double boiler 15 minutes, then add juice, rind and egg yolks and cook 5 more minutes. Let cool before pouring in crust.

Crust

1 1/2 cups flour
1/2 teaspoon salt
1/2 cup lard
(approximately)

Make paste of 1/4 cup flour and 3 tablespoons water. Mix above ingredients before adding the paste. Bake 10 to 18 minutes in 475 degree oven. Let cool before adding filling.

Meringue

Beat 3 egg whites and 2 tablespoons sugar until it forms peaks. Spread meringue on pie and bake in 325 degree oven from 15 to 20 minutes or until golden brown.

Georgia Coconut Pie

2 cups sugar
1 stick margarine
4 eggs
2 heaping tablespoons flour
1 cup milk
2 cups or more Angel
Flake coconut
2 teaspoons vanilla

Mix sugar, melted margarine, eggs and milk. Add coconut and vanilla. Pour into unbaked 9-inch pie shells. Bake 10 minutes at 450 degrees then turn to 375 degrees and bake until done. Makes two pies.

Prune Pudding Bread

1 cup vegetable oil
3 eggs
2 cups white sugar
Cream together.

2 cups flour
1 1/2 teaspoons cinnamon
1 teaspoon vanilla
1 teaspoon soda
1 teaspoon salt
1 cup buttermilk
1 cup prunes, cooled, seeded and mashed
1 tablespoon extra flour

Blend with mixer. Fold in 1 cup nuts. Bake in greased tube pan for 1 hour at 350 degrees. If you use other pans, fill 2/3 full. Let cool.

A good glass of *wine* deserves to be served in fine crystal.

Beverages

Break the Ice Punch

1 quart brandy
1 quart rum
1 quart sherry
1 quart vodka
2 cups sugar
juice of 8 lemons
1 to 2 bottles sparkling water

Cool first 4 ingredients and mix. Add sugar and lemon juice. Cool 3 to 4 hours. Add cold water just prior to serving.

Southern Punch

3 pounds sugar
2 ounces citric acid
2 quarts hot water
1-46 ounce can orange juice
1-46 ounce can pineapple juice
3 quarts cold water

Dissolve sugar in citric acid and hot water. Cool. Add remaining ingredients. Mix well. Makes 2 gallons.

Sunbowl Punch

4 cups hot, strong coffee
2 cups warm milk
1 cup bourbon
1 cup creme de cacao

Try on a cold winter night.

Lime Punch

1 large can pineapple juice
3 cans frozen limeade concentrate
1 can frozen lemonade concentrate
1/2 quart water
1 gallon lime sherbet
1 quart ginger ale
green food coloring

Add water to limeade and lemonade concentrate. Add chilled pineapple juice. Add a few drops of green food coloring. Pour into punch bowl and add softened sherbet; add cold ginger ale. Serves 30 to 40 people.

Jello Punch

1 package jello (any flavor)
1 large can pineapple juice
1 cup sugar
6 tablespoons lemon juice

Dissolve jello in 1 pint of hot water. Add sugar and juices. Add 1/2 gallon cold water. Yield: 1 gallon punch.

Party Punch

2 packages lemon-lime Kool Aid
2 quarts water
2 cups sugar
1 large can pineapple juice
1 quart ginger ale

Mix first four ingredients. Freeze. Remove from freezer about an hour before serving. Put in bowl and pour over 1 quart ginger ale.

Percolator Punch

1 quart cranberry juice
1-46 ounce can pineapple juice
1 quart cranapple juice
1 cup brown sugar
handful whole cloves
6 cinnamon sticks

In bottom of large percolator (30 cup) put: cranberry juice, pineapple juice, cranapple juice and brown sugar. In top basket, place cloves and cinnamon sticks. Percolate. This will not damage your coffee pot.

Wedding Punch

2 large cans fruit punch
3 quarts unsweetened pineapple juice
1-6 ounce can frozen orange juice
1-6 ounce can frozen lemon juice
1/2 cup sugar
6 large bottles ginger ale

Mix all ingredients in punch bowl. Chill with ice and serve. Can be mixed in batches ahead and chilled until ready for use. Serves 65.

from the kitchen of Lynette Wright

Patio Blush

1/2 cup frozen orange juice concentrate, thawed and undiluted
1/4 cup lemon juice
1/4 cup maraschino cherry juice
1/4 cup honey
28 ounces ginger ale, chilled
1 pint pineapple sherbet

Combine fruit juices and honey. Mix well. Pour equal amounts into 4 chilled glasses. Top each with pineapple sherbet. Serves 4.

How To Preserve A Husband

(found in grandmother's scrapbook)

Be careful in your selection. Do not choose too young, and take only such varieties as have been reared in a good moral atmosphere. When once decided upon and selected, let that part remain forever settled and give your entire thought to preparation for domestic use. Some insist on keeping them in a pickle, while others are constantly getting them into hot water. Even poor varieties may be made sweet, tender and good by garnishing them with patience, well sweetened with smiles and flavored with kisses. Then wrap well in a mantle of charity. Keep warm with a steady fire of domestic devotion and serve with the fruits of constant devotion and milk of human kindness. When thus prepared, they will keep for years. (We hope this gets desired results, which is to help women who have 'em to keep 'em and those who don't have 'em to get 'em and keep 'em well preserved.)

Perserving Children

1 large grassy field
6 children
3 small dogs
hot sun
flowers
deep blue sky
narrow strip of brook with pebbles

Mix the children with the dogs and empty into the field, stirring continously. Sprinkle the field with flowers; pour the brook over the pebbles. Cover all with a deep blue sky and bake it in a hot sun. When children are well browned, they may be removed. Will be found right for setting away to cool in bath tub.

Jellies, Jam & Pickles

My Family

When I look back on my family, laughter and joy abounds
Love, peace and happiness are things I've always found.

As I ponder each one's face and how they've changed with time
It's their voices I remember most as they often cross my mind.

My Uncle Bill's is stern and strong and sounds like no other
The flat talk of the mountain folk can be heard through my mother.

The excitement of Aunt Sharon has a tenor all it's own
And the high pitched tones of Aunt Rose allows her to be known.

Aunt Phoebe's voice is gentle and grows softer by the day
While Aunt Melanie's is bossy, saying do it all this way.

Though Mamaw and Sissy have moved on to a better place
I can still see both of them as I look upon each face.

My cousins, their spouse and their kids complete my family
I must be very special for God to give them all to me.

Each one is so precious, so loving and so kind
And my life is best spent with them, if only in my mind.

Tammy Shelton Wilson

Feed The Hungry Children

It's Christmas time in the neighborhood
And homes are filled with anticipation;
But in another neighborhood there's nothing there
But worry and frustration.
The wonderful aroma in the first neighborhood
Are pumpkin pies baking;
But in the other neighborhood
A mother's heart is breaking.
She stares at their scrap of tree
And is reminded each day their chances grow dimmer.
Dear Lord, what she'd give to only have
Her children Christmas dinner.
She opens up her Bible and reads about the birth of the King.
Little eyes all open wide as she begins to sing!
Then one by one they're all tucked in and prayers have all been said.
She prays, Dear Lord provide the flour so I can make them bread.
They see the families that are blessed and their hearts
are filled with yearning
But deep inside, through no fault of their own,
their stomachs with hunger are burning.
You and I can stop the pain, where there are tears
there can be endless joy.
When we feed the children, we can make it
Christmas year round for these girls and boys.

Sharon Strickland

Please contribute to your local Salvation Army,
so the hungry children can be fed.
Thank you,
Rose and Sharon

Brandied Cranberries

1 bag of cranberries
2 1/2 cups of sugar
2 3/4 cups water
1 package raspberry jello
1/2 cup pecans, chopped
1/3 cup brandy

Wash and pick stems off cranberries. Put in a large kettle; add sugar and water. Stir and cook until done. Add jello; stir well. Take off stove, cool, then add pecans plus brandy.

Hot Pepper Jelly

4 bell peppers, seeds removed
12 small green or red peppers, seeds removed
5 pounds sugar
3 cups white vinegar
2-6 ounce liquid pectin

Grind peppers in food chopper along with 1/3 cup water. Boil sugar and vinegar 5 minutes. Add pectin and boil 1 minute. Skim foam. Add drops of red or green coloring. Pour into sterlized jars and seal.

Brandied Cranberry Sauce

1 pound cranberries
2 cups sugar
1/2 cup brandy

Spread 1 pound of cranberries in a shallow baking dish. Sprinkle 2 cups of sugar over the cranberries. Cover tightly with foil. Bake for 1 hour. Cool for a few minutes. Remove foil and then add 1/2 cup or more of brandy. Stir and mix well. Store in refrigerator. Will last for several weeks.

Freezer Peach Jam

Wonderful fresh flavor
3 medium Georgia peaches
2 3/4 cups sugar
1/2 cup light corn syrup
1/2 teaspoon asorbic acid powder
3 ounces liquid fruit pectin
3 teaspoons lemon juice

Wash and pit peaches. Place in blender container and puree. Measure 1 cup puree. Add sugar, corn syrup and ascorbic acid and blend thoroughly. Allow to stand 10 minutes.

Add pectin and lemon juice and blend well. Pour into 1/2 pint freezer containers leaving 1/2-inch headspace. Cover with tight fitting lids. Let stand at room temperature 24 hours or until set. Place in freezer.

This jam does not freeze solidly and may be used directly from the freezer. Could also be stored up to two weeks in the refrigerator. Because no cooking is needed, it has that fresh peach flavor. Makes about 4 cups.

Peach and Cantaloupe Preserves

2 cups peaches
2 cups cantaloupe
3 cups sugar
1 lemon, juice and grated rind

Slice peaches. Cut cantaloupe into 3/4-inch cubes. Mix all and simmer on low until syrup forms. Cool slowly until syrup is thickened and fruit is clear. Let stand until cool. Put into sterilized jars and process in simmering water 10 minutes.

Vegetable Relish

8 carrots
12 green sweet peppers
2 red sweet peppers
2 red hot peppers
12 large onions
2 medium-size heads of cabbage

Grind all through the food chopper, sprinkle with salt (2 tablespoons). Mix thoroughly, and let stand 1 hour. Drain well.

Chow Chow

Cut into small bits the following vegetables:

carrots
cabbage
string beans
cauliflower
onions

use for color:

lima beans
corn
red kidney beans
small white beans

Salt to taste as they are cooked. Cut green tomatoes and green pepper into small bits but do not cook. Measure the mixture into a large container and mix with your hands.

For each gallon of vegetable mixture, boil together:

1 pint good vinegar
1 tablespoon celery seeds
6 cups sugar

Add the vegetables to the boiling sugar and vinegar and cook until the tomatoes and peppers are cooked. Seal in sterile jars while hot. Corn and lima beans may be fresh or frozen. Red kidney beans and string beans may be canned.

Mixed Corn Relish

1 teaspoon turmeric
1 teaspoon celery seed
2 tablespoons dry mustard
1/2 cup salt
2 cups light brown sugar
1 quart cider vinegar
12 ears yellow corn, cut from cob
1 medium head cabbage, finely shredded
4 medium white onions, finely diced
4 sweet green peppers, finely diced
4 sweet red peppers, finely diced

Mix spices, salt, sugar and vinegar. Combine with vegetables. Cook over low heat, about 1 hour, stirring occasionally until slightly thickened. Relish thickens as it cools. Pack while hot into sterilized jars. Seal at once. Yields: 20 cups.

Old Seed Cucumber Pickles

7 1/2 pounds cucumbers, peeled, seeded and cut in strips
2 gallons cold water
3 cups household lime

Mix the water and lime and pour over cucumbers; let stand 24 hours. Wash thoroughly until all lime is gone. Allow to stand in fresh cold water for 3 hours.

Mix together:
2 quarts vinegar
4 1/2 pounds sugar
1 tablespoon pickling spice

Let mixture come to a boil. Cool. Pour over cukes and let stand 12 hours. Cook over medium heat until clear. Seal in glass jars.

from the kitchen of Jane

Kosher Dill Pickles

In one quart jar put:
1 head fresh dill
2 to 3 cloves garlic (depending on size)
1 small red or green hot pepper (optional)

Select fresh, firm cucumbers. Wash and pack in jars.

Bring to a boil:
2 quarts water
1 quart distilled or cider vinegar
1 cup non-iodized salt

Pour hot solution over cucumbers and seal. Pickles will be ready in 3 to 4 weeks.

Three Day Cucumber Pickles

7 pounds unpeeled cucumbers
2 cups lime
2 gallons water

Mix lime and water. Add cucumbers. Let stand for 24 hours. Drain and rinse. Let stand in clear, cold water for 3 hours.

Syrup

2 quarts vinegar
4 1/2 pounds sugar
1 teaspoon salt
1 teaspoon whole cloves
1 teaspoon celery seed
1 teaspoon pickling spices

Mix. Add cucumbers. Let stand overnight. Boil 35 to 40 minutes. Put into sterlized jars and seal.

Candied Dill Pickles

1 quart commercially canned dill pickles
2 cups sugar
1 tablespoon vinegar
3 tablespoons pickling spice
1/4 cup pickling juice from jar

Drain (reserve 1/4 cup juice). In large non-aluminum container add sugar, vinegar, spices and juice; stir. Slice pickles in half lengthwise. Place halves in mixture and stir. Let stand until all sugar is absorbed. Return pickle halves to original jar and pour liquid over pickles. Cover and seal. Refrigerate 3 to 4 days before serving.

Squash Pickle

Cut into thin slices 10 or 12 unpeeled yellow squash and 3 large onions. Put into brine of one gallon water and 1 cup salt. Soak 12 hours. Drain 1 hour.

Put into kettle:

5 cups vinegar
2 cups sugar
1 cup water
1 teaspoon turmeric
1/2 cup brown sugar
2 tablespoons mustard seed
1 tablespoon celery seed

Boil this mixture for 5 minutes. Add squash and simmer 2 to 3 minutes. Bring to a boil, pack in hot jars and seal.

Refrigerator Pickles

7 cups sliced unpeeled cucumbers
1 cup sliced onions
1 cup sliced green pepper
1 tablespoon celery seed
2 cups sugar
1 cup vinegar

Mix together and store in covered container in refrigerator. Add hot pepper, if desired.

Okra Pickle

Wash tender okra pods leaving caps on. Fill jars with okra.

For each pint use:
1 teaspoon dill seed
1 hot red pepper
1 hot green pepper
2 cloves garlic

Bring to boil 1 quart vinegar, 1/2 cup uniodized salt, and 1 cup water. When mixture boils, pour over okra in jars then seal and let stand 2 weeks. Chill before serving.

Green Tomato Pickle

6 pints green tomatoes, cut up
6 pints cabbage, shredded
3 pints sweet red peppers, cut up
3 pints sweet green peppers, cut up
5 pints onions, cut up

Put all through meat grinder, sprinkle liberally with salt, put in a bag and let hang overnight to drain.

3 tablespoons mixed spices, tied in a bag
2 teaspoons mustard seed, loose
2 teaspoons celery seed, loose

Put all ingredients in large kettle, add 3 quarts strong vinegar and 3 quarts water, plus 8 3/4 cups white sugar; bring to boil and cook slowly for about 1 hour, watching closely to keep from scorching. Seal hot in sterile jars. Makes 14 pints.

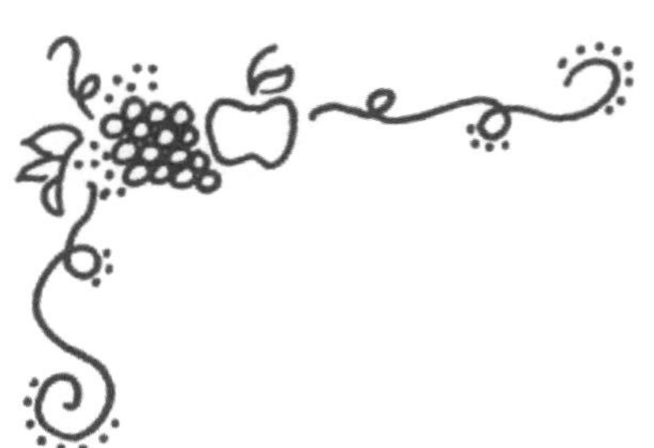

jellies, jams & pickles

Stories & Poems

from our hearts
to yours

Stories
are
made to be
told to
others.

SOUFFLE

5 eggs
5 tablespoons milk
1/4 teaspoon white pepper
3 slices sour dough or french bread, cubed
3/4 cup cheddar cheese, grated

Scramble eggs and milk; add pepper. Spray 4 ramekin dishes.

Arrange bread cubes into the dishes and cover each with equal amounts of cheese. Pour equal amounts of egg mixture over each. Cover with cling wrap and refrigerate overnight. Bake at 375 degrees fro 23 to 28 minutes. Souffles should rise and have a golden top. Remove and serve warm with toast. Be creative using different cheeses, or add browned breakfast meats or turn a little tex-mex flair with chili and salsa.

from the kitchen of Judith Frampton,
Prospect Hill Bed & Breakfast
Waynesville, North Carolina

Our stay in our hometown, while putting together this book, was made more special by staying with Judith and Dennis Frampton of Prospect Hill Bed & Breakfast in Waynesville, North Carolina. The flowers were in full bloom and the gardens were so beautiful. We have decided that Dennis makes the best souffles around, we hope to return soon to the beautiful house on the hill.

Rose and Sharon

Southern Ladies

Southern Ladies are
such a treat,
That's because they're
so sweet.
Wearing long dresses,
hats and gloves,
Having tea parties for
people they love.
The way that they cook for all
that are dear,
Makes me want to stand up
and cheer!
For all the memories with
grace and class,
Manners for them will
always last.

"Lucy E"
Edwina Burch
My Secret Garden
Orlando, Florida

Believe

A while back one of our neighbors had a hobby shop in a small building on our property. He cut sayings and numbers into beautiful flat river rock, such as addresses and inspirationals for flower beds.

One day our two young granddaughters, Sydney 10 and Sarah 6, came to visit for the day. Our yard is totally fenced in so I felt reasonably comfortable leaving them unattended while I finished up pressing paperwork.

As I worked I listened to the little voices squabbling, laughing and telling stories. A comfort and peace settled over me as my work became more involved.

A short while later my niece, Tammy, came in and asked what the girls were in to. I suddenly realized things had become too quite.

As we headed out the door we noticed on a board in big white painted letters, the name, SARAH! We rounded the house and again on another board in the same lettering, SARAH!

Fearing the worst we tracked the girls down to the hobby shop. On the outside sliding door, again, SARAH, but this work of art also told she had been there.

Suddenly they were there before us; hands

continued on page 194

covered with white paint. Sydney's more so. I believe she had been there more than Sarah had.

While cleaning hands, there were the usual threats, "Wait 'til your pappaw sees this and your moms get here." During this time one accused the other.

After they went home and their work of vandalism was taken care of, I decided to take a break. With a glass of iced tea in hand, I strolled back the same paths they had taken. Something white caught my eye, I bent over and picked up a beautiful flat river stone, painted white, with the word, Believe, carved into it. A remnant from our neighbors left over hobby, and a true masterpiece of art from our little granddaughters, frozen in time.

To this day I still have that rock. It sits in a place of prominance on my desk. When things seem to be closing in, with deadlines and commitments, I look at this solid rock and feel rejuvinated, strong and again I do Believe!

Sharon Strickland, 2002

God, What Do I Say Now?

My little granddaughter called the other day,
and I could tell she was deeply troubled right away.

So with a happy front, I tried to lighten the mood
by saying the holidays are coming!
Doesn't that sound good?

A heavy silence filled my ear.
then a little voice choked with tears.

My next question was, my sweet child,
Tell me what's wrong
The answer I dreaded most didn't take long.

You know, she responded, I hate this time of year
It was my turn to sit in silence as my heart broke
listening to her fears.

You see, her mom and dad divorced in January, two years past.
A rock solid marriage everyone thought would last.

Then in a small voice she asked, "Memaw, what can I do?"
I want to be with my daddy, but I want my mom too.

I searched for words of comfort, so hard to find,
Though a million of them tumbled in my mind.

I could feel her torment as she went on to explain
I just wish things could be like they used to be again.

I tried so hard to help her and to make her see,
I quickly pointed out,
she still had her mom, dad, pappaw and me.

continued on page 196

And others were sent to share her life and with this
she had truly been blessed.
I asked her if she understood,
and got a thoughtful, " I guess."

With the usual, "I love you", we hung up the phones.
And suddenly I knew the total feeling,
like her, of being alone.

I sat and thought for a while knowing, in years to come,
she would be all right some how.
But in my mind I wondered,
"God, what do I say right now?"

Sharon Strickland

Birthday Wishes

The night before my birthday
I worried about growing old,
The bloom of youth had faded,
No more precious babies to hold.
In deep thought I drifted back
to years that had gone by
Amid silently, I asked myself,
what was the purpose and why?
Was it to see the young girl, then young woman,
that I used to be?
Or was it just my memories,
making fun of me?
A wrinkle here, a sag there,
I couldn't find that young woman anywhere!
As night gave way to morning,
I was still wide awake.
Maybe no one would remember,
And keep quite for my sake.
The day progressed as slowly,
I thought night would never come.
Then the door burst open,
In came my only son.
Then one by one they all came,
In with presents and birthday wishes,
Birthday cake was happily served,
Afterwards, my daughters did the dishes.

continued on page 198

As time had gone slowly,
It was now moving too fast.
I was back in the present
Not thinking of the past
Precious hugs and kisses from grandbabies
as I walked them to the door
Then in unison my daughters asked,
"Mom what did you wish for?"
I stood there trying to find the right words
as I stared at the grown women and the man,
My son stepped toward me and asked,
"Mom, are you allright?"
As he gently took my hand.
Then clearly as the sun breaks over the darkened hill,
I understood God's purpose and
His mighty will.
A chuckle rose in my throat as
I realized this is how he meant for things to be,
For through my children
I could see my youth staring back at me.

Sharon A. Strickland

The Old Camp Meeting Came To Town

The tent meeting is comin! The tent meeting is comin!
There's excitement all around.
They paid us kids fifty cents to hang posters around town.
The posters said, "Camp Meeting In Chestnut Park."
Bring your families and friends and meet our new reverend, Mark.
Now, reverend Mark was quite a man to behold.
His beard was white and looked like Santa, I was told.
The meeting took place exactly at seven o'clock.
You could hear our reverend Mark for at least ten blocks.
He preached on sin and how we all should live,
And he asked for 10% and said we all should give.
Lou La Bell was caught up in the spirit of things,
She shouted all night, my God, she could let it ring.
Us kids were given a nickle and sometimes a dime,
To sing a few hymns while our uncles picked and kept time.
Mama served grape KoolAid and passed it all around,
As the preacher picked it up and slammed a few down,
The day the old camp meeting came to town.

Rose

The Day The Old Outhouse came down

Today's the day the outhouse is coming down
I could hardly sleep from excitement going around.
The men dug a big hole on the other side of the hill,
I can't remember who was more excited, myself or Bill.
As the neighborhood watched with anticipation,
A wonder was built that fired our imagination.
The building was bigger and the wood looked brand new,
We opened the door, and my God, there was two!
Two holes cut out so perfectly round,
In case of company coming to town.
The excitement of the day is one I'll never forget,
This new invention was fun and I'll bet,
The new Sears and Roebuck Catalog would soon be out,
And they left a place in the middle to spread it about.
The old outhouse was soon a thing of the past,
As our neighbors soon built one as fancy as,
The one I'll remember throughout eternity,
The two-seater designed for you and for me.

Rose

Recipes

Recipes

Recipes

Recipes

Reorder Additional Copies

MAILTO:

204 East Bay Street
Savannah, GA 31401

Please mail copy(ies) of your cookbook @ $15.95 each _______

Postage & Packaging @ $2.00 each _______

Georgia residents please add 6%sales tax _______

Mail books to:

Name ____

Address ____

City, State, Zip ________________________________

Published by Rosemary Arrington Newman and Sharon Arrington Strickland
Printed By Square One Graphics, Inc. Jacksonville, Florida

- -

MAILTO:

Tomorrow May Never Come So... Lets Eat it ALL Today

204 East Bay Street
Savannah, GA 31401

Please mail copy(ies) of your cookbook @ $15.95 each _______

Postage & Packaging @ $2.00 each _______

Georgia residents please add 6%sales tax _______

Mail books to:

Name ____

Address ____

City, State, Zip ________________________________

Published by Rosemary Arrington Newman and Sharon Arrington Strickland
Printed By Square One Graphics, Inc. Jacksonville, Florida

APPETIZERS, SOUPS & SALADS

SAUCES & DRESSINGS

SAUCES & DRESSINGS (continued)

VEGETABLES

index

MAIN COURSES & CASSEROLES

SEAFOOD

BREADS

COOKIES & CANDY

DESSERTS

DESSERTS (continued)

index

BEVERAGES

JELLIES, JAMS & PICKLES

POEMS & SHORT STORIES

POEMS & STORIES (continued)